D0997175

MENUHIN
A Family Portrait

MENUHIN

A Family Portrait

TONY PALMER

faber and faber

LONDON · BOSTON

First published in 1991
by Faber and Faber Limited
3 Queen Square London WC1N 3AU

Photoset by Butler & Tanner Ltd, Frome and London
Printed in England by Clays Ltd, St Ives plc

© Isolde Films Ltd, 1991

Tony Palmer is hereby identified as author of this work
in accordance with Section 77 of the Copyright, Designs and
Patents Act 1988

A CIP record for this book
is available from the British Library
ISBN 0–571–16582–6

Contents

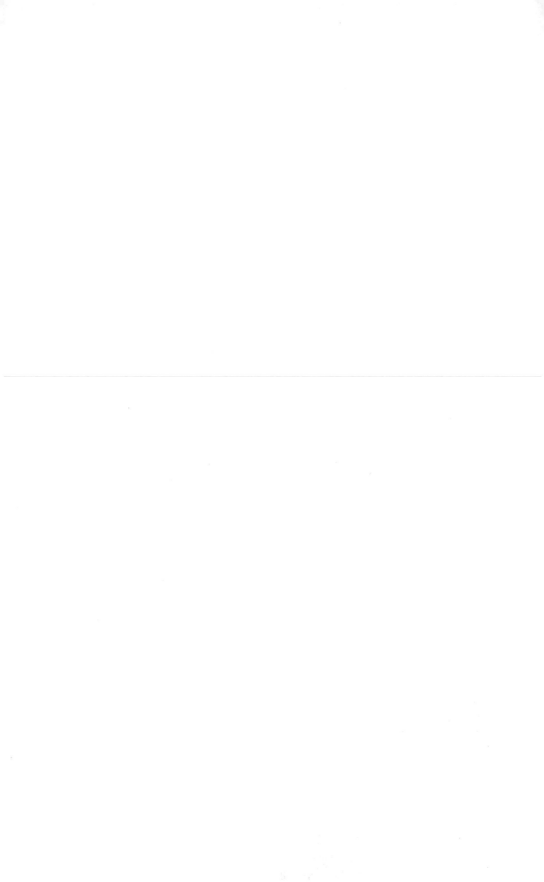

Illustrations

Pictures 1–20 are reproduced by permission of The Hulton Picture Company; picture 21 appears by permission of Tony Palmer.

Preface

The text for this book arose from materials I collected while making a television biography of Sir Yehudi Menuhin. The film, which was also subtitled 'A Family Portrait', was researched over three years, and I am aware that the broadcast version contains only a small part of what I am able to include here. Of course, what a book cannot include is the sound of Sir Yehudi's playing, without which it might be argued no biography of Menuhin is complete.

I am especially grateful to those who encouraged me to make the film, particularly Reiner Moritz, Melvyn Bragg and Colin Leventhal. Without Chris Cook and Grindlays /ANZ Bank, and their financial support, moreover, the film would never have been made. It was first transmitted on Channel Four Television in Britain, to celebrate Sir Yehudi's seventy-fifth birthday.

What follows, therefore, is not biography in the strictest sense, although it gives the illusion of chronology, and all its facts, as far as I can ascertain, are correct. Rather, it is an impression of the man and his artistry through the words – principally – of his family, living or dead. No expert musical opinion was sought, and none is included. A day by day, or even month by month, diary of events is not part of this impression.

I believe my interpretation of all that I was told by the family is truthful, and in so far as the book – like the film – has no particular viewpoint, at least not to the exclusion of all others, I feel confident that a degree of objectivity has been maintained.

Any researcher into the life of Sir Yehudi is indebted first to his own thorough autobiography, *Unfinished Journey*, first published in 1977 by Macdonald and Jane's, from which I have taken much information and reminiscences. Likewise, Robert Magidoff's biography, *Yehudi Menuhin*, first published in 1956 by Robert Hale & Co., is indispensable. Scrupulously fair, and accurate in so far as Menuhin himself approved the text, Magidoff's work provided me again with many anecdotes and numerous quotations. Sir Yehudi's own archivist, Jutta Schall-Emden, and his secretary Vera Lamport, have been tireless in their efforts to keep me on the right track.

I must report that Sir Yehudi and Lady Menuhin did not entirely approve of the television film, and requested that several passages be changed, some because of incorrect facts, others because of what they argued were matters of incorrect emphasis. I corrected all matters of fact, but I have no doubt that they will still find passages in this work distasteful.

All the interviews conducted by me and contained herein were either tape-recorded or accompanied by copious note-taking. I have only adjusted the grammar to make sense of the written word as opposed to the rhythms of spoken dialogue. In addition, all the Menuhins frequently refer to Mrs Menuhin Senior by her Jewish familiar name as 'Mammina' or 'Imma'; likewise to Mr Menuhin Senior as 'Aba'. I have changed these references throughout to 'Marutha' and 'Moshe', their given names, for clarity. Thanks also to Christopher Falkus and Allegra Huston, and to my assistant Sally Reynolds who deciphered my scrawl. To my constant inspiration, well, she knows who that is.

You cannot make a film biography, or write a book such as this, without finishing up loving your subject. I don't really expect any members of the Menuhin family who might come across this book to believe me. But my admiration (and love) for Sir Yehudi grew profoundly during the making of the film and the writing of the book. It has been a privilege to know him and work with him. If what follows is not hagiography, then he would be the first to accept that it could not be so. After watching the film, he merely said: 'It's time it all came out.'

Nanjizal, 28 July 1991

I

Childhood

In his autobiography Yehudi Menuhin writes that his 'early years shine . . . as a time of untarnished happiness'. It is undoubtedly this belief which has sustained him throughout his long and extraordinary life, even when tragedy stalked him at the door and mercilessly unbalanced his state of well-being. For never was a man so committed, in a very public way, to the well-being of others, to the well-being of his family, and to the well-being of himself. That the man is humble is clear; that the man is gifted, both as a musician and as a benefactor, is equally clear; that the man is the child of the father and the father of the child, is not only also clear but has been devastating in its consequences. Within the man hides the child, whose early years were not a time of unblemished happiness, but often of unremitting agony. This is the story of a man whose childhood betrayed him, yet who, even now, in his seventy-fifth year, cannot face that understanding.

Few of us can, of course, but Menuhin has so persistently made a virtue out of his blameless childhood that it comes as a shock to realize that the truth is somewhat different. His younger sister told me: 'One felt as if no one was there [to help]. You could knock and knock [at the door of the "family"]. But it was like a prison door. A door made of stone. You could knock and knock and nothing would happen, except you would hurt your knuckles. Every child goes through a period of great need, of feeling someone should be there. If not a mother, then a teacher or a friend or a relative. In our case, no one was ever there.'

Yehudi Menuhin was born on 22 April 1916. The Menuhins were Russian; the father, Moshe, came from Gomel, in the centre of the Pale, between the Baltic and the Black Sea. The mother, Marutha Sher, came from the Crimea, near Yalta. Both families emigrated to Palestine, where Moshe and Marutha first met. But it was not until Moshe and Marutha had separately moved on to New York that their relationship blossomed into marriage. When their first-born arrived, Marutha was just twenty. He was named Yehudi, the Jew, an act of defiance against a New York landlady on the Lower East Side who had attempted to persuade the Menuhins to rent her apartment with the observation: 'You know, of course, that I never take Jews.' How anyone could have looked at Moshe or at the pregnant Marutha and not realized they were Jews is not immediately apparent. But it's a good story, and Yehudi tells it often.

Moshe's antecedents were Hassidic, the dancing and violin-playing Jews who supplied music and entertainment at weddings and other festivities. The Menuhins were also a hereditary rabbinate, and Menuhin senior grew up in Jerusalem wearing 'those rather deforming side whiskers' (according to his son), 'bent his head in reverent prayers and studied through the night, every night'. Not surprisingly, Moshe rebelled and, aged only fourteen, tried to get a visa to America. Having got as far as Marseilles, he was told by the American consulate he was too young, and, by the way, where were his parents? He was sent packing, back to Palestine, but not before he had managed to spend a day in Paris. A boy of fourteen? With, presumably, not too much money, despite a gift of one hundred dollars from his grandfather? Five hundred kilometres to the north? A day trip? Again, it's a good story, and Yehudi tells it often, although the exact age at which his father embarked upon this great enterprise does vary according to the occasion.

Yehudi claims his mother was a Tartar in every sense of the word.

Strong-minded, self-disciplined, wild at times, but – according to her son – 'never vindictive, never hard, but always very, *very* strong; wouldn't tolerate fools, wouldn't even tolerate some wise people who crossed her path. I've never seen her bend. I've never embraced her but that I felt a corset around her. As straight-backed as anyone could be.' She was the only surviving child of seven, whose father had abandoned her and her mother in the Crimea. In 1911, when Marutha was fifteen, mother and daughter moved to Jaffa. Less than a year later (again according to Yehudi), she travelled to Kiev, London, Moscow, Manchester and the United States with the intention of 'visiting relatives'.

Mother and daughter (in what little remaining time must have been left them) spoke Tartar, and believed themselves to be descendants of the Tartari khans. Marutha's hero was a Circassian warrior, a sort of Eastern Sir Lancelot, and every home she subsequently made with Moshe retained an Oriental flavour. She would receive friends dressed in silken Turkish trousers, fastened round her extremely tiny waist with a silver belt. Exotic rugs were everywhere, a cushion-laden divan always placed by the garden window. All her children remember the family living room having the atmosphere (and the privacy) of a harem, in which their father (among many others) was not particularly welcome. Public photographs of the children with their mother are rare indeed. Such things would not have been tolerated in the harem.

Indeed, the *Arabian Nights* soon became favourite and essential reading for the boy Yehudi. After all, Yehudi told me, the Orient was 'a fabulous land whose beauties no other country could match'. And the most beautiful of Oriental beauties was undoubtedly Marutha. Even today, her high cheekbones and flashing smile totally dominate any gathering. As far as one can tell from the photographs, when she was a young woman in her twenties she had a radiant, almost ethereal beauty. She had dazzling blue eyes, and she was only five feet two inches tall.

Moshe had found a job in New York teaching Hebrew; indeed,

until Yehudi's arrival, he had seemed destined for an academic life. He had finally come to New York as a result of a mathematics scholarship to New York University in the Bronx, and soon became principal of the Talmud Torah in Elizabeth, New Jersey. But neither Moshe nor Marutha were in any sense orthodox Jews. As Yehudi describes it, the Jews of Elizabeth might just as well have been living in the Pale of Poland. By contrast, his parents were Chalutzim, that is 'Palestinian pioneers', for whom Hebrew was a necessary form of communication rather than a sacred tongue. (Hebrew was Yehudi's first language.)

For Moshe, 'the deader the language, the better'. Such an attitude did not endear him to the Chief Rabbi; nor did what were described as Marutha's 'outrageous sense of dress' and 'scandalously bobbed hair'. 'My father was a very sensual man,' Yehudi told me. 'And passionate. Passionate in his loves and his hates. He was a glutton for ice cream, and once claimed to have given himself appendicitis by eating fourteen helpings of ice cream at one sitting. But he was also a great idealist, a pioneer rather than a parishioner. A bound edition of Karl Marx sat comfortably on his bookshelves next to the Talmud. He adored America, and what he perceived as its freedoms, and his dream was to have a house with a garden of its own.' Later, when his dream had been fulfilled at the family home in Los Gatos, California, Moshe became inordinately proud of his avocados and tomatoes and plums and oranges and an abundance of flowers. No man, it seems, could have been happier. He had created, remembered Yehudi, 'his own Israel, his own Jerusalem'. One can understand why he always referred later in life to Elizabeth, New Jersey, as 'Elizabethdump'.

After two years in Elizabeth, Moshe could take it no more. Guilt, exile and lamentation as practised by the local Jews were not for him. A newspaper article about the opportunities available in California caught his eye, and within a week the family were off. Alas, at Grand Central Station in New York, they discovered that even the cheapest journey across the continent of the United States would cost fifteen dollars more than they had. We must presume it was the pathetic sight of two refugees, baggage, and a squealing two-year-old Yehudi which inspired the ticket inspector to provide the balance. But this he did, and so the unnamed ticket inspector became Yehudi's 'first benefactor'.

Moshe already had a brother in California who ran a chicken farm, and had sent him a telegram advising him of their impending arrival. The brother duly met them at Oakland Pier and the Menuhins soon settled at 732 Hayes Street, with Moshe teaching Hebrew in the San Francisco Jewish Community at a salary of one hundred and fifty dollars per month. And although he was soon superintendent of all the Hebrew schools in the Bay Area, for once the family were careful to observe the niceties of Jewish community life. Only Yehudi, it seems, was less than careful. On one occasion they were offered corned beef at the local rabbi's house. 'Oh,' said Yehudi, 'that's not like our corned beef! Our corned beef is pink, and has stripes of nice white fat around it.'

Yehudi was four when his sister Hephzibah was born: Hephzibah 'the desired one', 'the longed-for one', which was 'just what she turned out to be, what was contracted for', Yehudi told me. A year and a half later, another sister 'completed the family'. She was named Yaltah, after the town on the Black Sea from which her mother came, a town which was to achieve notoriety after the Second World War. Even the dogs (Alupka, Alushta) were named after Circassian towns, and the home at 1043 Steiner Street to which the growing Menuhin family now moved – large enough to house the 'completed family' – soon resembled an Eastern bazaar, more fitting perhaps for a migrating tribe who just happened to have pitched tent in San Francisco. Turkish rugs, Persian carpets, bed-rooms without curtains so that the family rose and slept with the sun, even an awning pitched against a flat roof on the back of the house in which the children were encouraged to live 'if the weather was in any way suitable'. The memory of the 'icy thrill of cold sheets on foggy nights' stayed with Yehudi for years. And also the conviction that 'so dependent were my parents on each other, and so well-established their different functions, [that] there was no opportunity for discussion'.

'Our father cut our toenails and our fingernails,' Yaltah told me. 'And if we didn't feel well, he would cuddle us. But for the most part, one didn't cry; one didn't get upset. If one was sick, well, that's too bad. You just went on anyway. We were never allowed the luxury of feeling bad, or not wanting to do something.' 'I think what little warmth there was in our childhood came from Yehudi,' Hephzibah told a BBC reporter towards the end of her life. 'Mother was always too busy organizing our well-being, and Father attending the needs of Mother.' 'We all worshipped Mother,' Yaltah said. 'My father worshipped her, and he wanted us to worship her. And we tried. It comes very naturally to worship people when you're young. We always try to feel that way about someone. But one should have a chance to select the *object* of one's worship. One can convert, of course. And one can also learn a religion. And one should. Alas, we never did. If we had been tougher children, we probably would have said, "That's enough of that." And we might have stopped it. As it was, we even took the San Francisco fog seriously, for instance. We really thought the fog was part of God's plan for us, and so we had to bear it. And so we resorted to inner vision. We had our dream world, which was wonderful. It's still very hard to get *out* of that dream world. And in times of trouble, that's the world one does go into, the inner world. Because the outer world is collapsing.'

'I can't remember a time when pleasure outings did not enliven our weeks like so many bursts of sunshine,' Yehudi told me. Certainly one can imagine the joy of growing up in the California of the early twenties. If San Francisco was not Hollywood, it seems to have had the same spirit of endless adventure and enterprise at this time. Every turn, every day, brought fresh horizons. Smog had not drenched the atmosphere; the Napa Valley, from where the best American wines were soon to come, was a Garden of Eden. And in any case, San Francisco was, and remains, one of the most fascinating, beautiful and culturally diverse cities on earth.

And Moshe was never without an eye for the main chance. He soon converted the basement of their new house on Steiner Street into a mini-garage, capable of housing seven cars! The space was, of course, rented out at six dollars a month per car, which more than paid for the monthly mortgage payments on the house, and bought the family a Chevrolet. Yehudi at other times says that the Chevrolet was bought with what was left over from money sent by his mother's mother to purchase his first violin. Either way, the family clearly adored the Chevrolet, not least because it was the means by which to explore northern California. And it was in the back seat of this Chevrolet that Yehudi experienced a moment of truth whose consequences have been profound. Yehudi, who was already having violin lessons, was waiting for Hephzibah to come out of a house where she was having a piano lesson. Adjacent was a food store, with people going in and out, buying food, and going about their 'normal daily tasks'. Yehudi realized, he recounted later, that for him these simple daily tasks were henceforward to be shunned and avoided forever as 'preposterous' and 'meaningless'.

The Chevrolet became a symbol of all that was meaningful. It took the happy family (at fifteen miles an hour!) to the Santa Clara Valley, 'a bed of blossom in springtime'; to the icy refuge of Lake Tahoe; to the Santa Cruz mountains, 'not high but romantically wooded'; and to a village called The Holy City – with Moshe all the while singing (according to Yehudi) the haunting, wordless songs of the Hassidic tradition. This four-door Chevy convertible opened up 'ideal landscapes in my mind which nothing later was to overlay', Yehudi remembers, finding land 'untouched by human foot ... [which] sowed the seed for all my adult enthusiasms for a world embracing all creation, human, animal, vegetable and mineral'.

It is, of course, a wonderfully romantic view of a world long gone, when the summers were always hot, the winters always cold, the Christmases whiter, and youth eternal.

Yaltah told me: 'We never took walks in the park just to see the park. We always had books in our pockets; we were always studying *something*. Even now, almost seventy years later,' she said, 'if I go to the local supermarket, I always take a book with me in case I have to stand around in a queue, in the mistaken belief that only if I have a book in my hand will life be tolerable.'

'But surely a child should be allowed to learn one thing at a time?' Yaltah asked me. 'In our family, there was constant pressure. Preparing a lesson, memorizing good behaviour, learning a new language, adjusting to the language of the land we happened to find ourselves in. Later, when we were all touring with Yehudi, we were *always* carrying the key of a hotel room. Even meal-times were never simply meal-times. As the years went by and we became teenagers, our childhood habit of gathering round the meal table to discuss everything that had happened to us, persisted. We were only allowed to open our mail, for instance, at meal-times. Of course, children love to have some private area, or some relationship, all their own. But in our case, all our letters had to be read aloud to each other before we were allowed to eat. They were mostly letters from teachers or relations, mostly quite superficial letters in fact. They certainly weren't romantic letters; Mother never had to check on our virtue. But somehow you felt that, because of this public reading, the purity of the message had been tampered with. You were so embarrassed, so self-conscious, that the real meaning of the letter was lost. And big decisions were made at table in the same way. So-and-so didn't exist any more; so-and-so wasn't such a bad teacher – let's give them another chance. All sorts of political manœuvres that children ought not to have to think about. They ought *not* to have to look at things that way. Not to be contaminated in that way. It deprives them of their real innocence, and forces them to run to their inner sense for safety.'

School education was not obligatory in California in the 1920s.

Yehudi attended the local school for just one day, when he was six. Hephzibah survived for five days. Yaltah never went to school. Moshe and Marutha decided they could do better at home. A host of private tutors were engaged, tutors in foreign languages, history and geography. Indeed, most of Yaltah's earliest memories are of 'teachers coming and going'. The consequence, of course, was that the three children were effectively cut off from other children.

Yehudi, at least, appears to have few regrets about this. Moshe, Yehudi remembered, 'devoured' newspapers on Yehudi's behalf: the *New York Times*, the *Jewish Newsletter* and especially *The Nation*, a left-wing publication whose editor, Osward Garrison Villard, became one of Moshe's heroes. Moshe would cut out items of interest and make sure that Yehudi read them, a habit which continued right up until Moshe's death in 1981. The daughters received the same treatment, as a result of which (for instance) they grew up 'ignorant of all the domestic arts'. Cooking remains a mystery for Yaltah to this day, although she is an excellent hostess. 'Childhood is such a short time,' Yaltah remembers wistfully. Yehudi has often told her (she claims) that, in retrospect, he can now see that 'as children they were never really children. Only now, when they had reached over three score years, were they each discovering what they had missed. Only now could they safely be children for the rest of their lives.' There are those in the family who maintain that Yaltah has been 'playing this one-string fiddle all her life, and it's about time she stopped whining and grew up'. Perhaps Yaltah's bitterness about her own upbringing has so clouded her memory that any rational view of what happened is now difficult for her. There is not the slightest admission of any of this in Yehudi's autobiography.

Confined within 1043 Steiner Street, on a hill above the city, it appears that Yehudi only made the shortest of forays into the outside world without his parents. Once, in my presence, Marutha told Yehudi that she had never *forbidden* him to read *Mother Goose* or any other such 'silly stories'. Yehudi had just never been interested.

'No, that's not true,' Yehudi retorted, to Marutha's evident astonishment. 'I remember a short span when I used to read Sunday
comics,' he told her. 'You *did?*' she replied in mock astonishment.
'Well, only about three or four times,' Yehudi said, quickly and
apologetically. 'Then you must have had a private understanding
with your *father*,' the old lady said. 'No, no,' said Yehudi. 'It was a
private initiative.' '*Completely* your own?' she enquired defiantly.
'*Completely* private initiative,' said Yehudi.

An uncomfortable silence followed this exchange. Finally,
Marutha asked: 'But did you *understand* them?' Yehudi seemed
unsure how to reply. After some hesitation he said: 'Well, there was
one about a father who always got into trouble . . . something about
life with father.' Marutha did not react. The silence became ever
more difficult, until eventually Yehudi admitted: 'Yes, it was very
naughty. But . . .' The old lady pounced, and to me she said: 'You
see, I *said* he was mischievous.' 'I wanted to catch you out,' Yehudi
said to his mother who now glared at him, her son, her eldest child.
A mere seventy-plus years old, but still referred to as 'child'. 'And
premeditated,' she said to him defiantly. 'Life with father, was it?'

In everything he has written and said, Yehudi presents the
relationship between his parents as secure and loving. There was, at
the beginning, a certain pragmatism about the marriage; two young
refugees, virtually alone in New York who decided 'it was cheaper
living together than separately.' And, as Yehudi's exceptional talent
manifested itself and the parents realized that it was to be their life's
task to protect and foster this talent, Moshe and Marutha were
inevitably drawn closer and closer together in a common pursuit.

I'm not saying that theirs was not true love; I have no way of
knowing, one way or another. But the memories of their three
children are clearly at odds. Yehudi: 'There was a coherence in
family life which allowed all manner of speculations on the purpose
of the universe without threatening the fabric of existence.'
Hephzibah: 'From the first, we were imbued with a sense of purpose
in all things, a seriousness which precluded, for instance, the existence

of toys. We had no toys, as far as I recall, and while my father could see no harm in them, my mother made sure that any such entertainments which my father might smuggle into the house were automatically banished. This caused much tension between them.' And Yaltah?

'My mother used to say to me: "I picked a very good father for you." I remember thinking, even at the time, that it took away the respect she had for his masculinity, for his part in our family life, for his responsibility. Watching my parents, I realized that in this family one *didn't* feel. Mother never felt; that was clear. I came to believe that she was sitting on a tremendous accumulation of resentment against my father, and she took it out on me because I looked like him, and she loved the other two because they were more like her. To her, being married without love wasn't such a tragedy. In the Middle Ages, it wasn't a tragedy either. People were just married off. Fathers married their daughters to the princes of other lands. And never forget that my mother came from a society that was in many respects straight out of the Middle Ages.' Marutha never forgot, for instance, that her own grandfather had been killed by a mob while attempting to defend a poor Jew about to be lynched.

It would be a mistake, perhaps, to argue that Yehudi was so traumatized by his childhood that he was scarred for life. There is no reason to doubt his vision of a golden few years in San Francisco. After all, as Yehudi's own son Krov pointed out to me, Moshe and Marutha had no data, no ground rules. 'They couldn't go to a bookshelf and pull out a book on How to Bring Up a Genius. Or How to Bring Up a Child like Yehudi. There *were* no children like Yehudi. I am sure Marutha tried to do the best she could,' Krov continued. 'And her way of doing the best was to believe that she knew best, and the best was to isolate Yehudi. He must be polished like a gem. Expose him only to those influences which are going to enhance the value of this human being and bring forth his genius.

'But the disadvantage of this method was that – paradoxically

– as a human being Yehudi was totally unprepared for real, normal life,' Krov told me. 'If Yehudi threw a tantrum, it could go on for days. He'd lock himself in a room and sulk, merely if something displeased him. And it is clear to me that in her efforts to protect Yehudi, Marutha neglected the other two children. Neither Hephzibah nor Yaltah can be said to have lived fulfilled lives. Yaltah appears to have suffered most, which is not surprising, when you remember that Marutha had wanted another son. When Yaltah turned out to be a girl, and what's more bearing a striking physical resemblance to her father, she was simply put in a closet whenever the important task of looking after Yehudi was threatened.' Yaltah, nicknamed by Marutha 'Jerusalem', has not seen her mother for the last thirty years.

For Yehudi, especially after his interest in the violin had been awakened, no parental attention was too much. Life in 1043 Steiner Street followed a strict pattern. Up at seven, breakfast, bath and practice until eleven. An hour for 'healthy outdoor exercise'. Lunch, possibly a picnic on the beach, followed by lessons for two hours from three o'clock. Half past five and another hour's practice. Tea, and in bed by seven. As Yehudi admits, although the bedtime hour 'eventually' stretched to nine, except on concert days this was his life from age four until his early teens. Day in, day out, with scarcely any deviation, except for holidays in the Chevy. Even the hour of 'healthy outdoor exercise' was 'never trespassed on by other duties', since Marutha considered it essential to the children's 'moral and spiritual make-up'. Most telling of all, perhaps, the three little children were encouraged to invent their own variety of tag, whose rules (says Yehudi) moulded 'the simple business of flight, pursuit and capture into a perfect logarithm table of points lost and won'.

Yehudi was five when Yaltah was born, in October 1921, and had already begun giving concerts. By the time Yaltah was five, Yehudi had begun touring; or to be more accurate, the family had begun touring. Due to an extraordinary series of benefactions (to which I shall return later), money was found to keep the family together, and before long San Francisco was left far behind. 'As a result, we weren't burdened with a household, or the mechanics of it,' Yaltah told me. 'It was like being a bird in flight. And there were always, here and there, kind souls who made us feel the world had all sorts of possibilities. Mother used to call people "Aunt So-and-so", or "Uncle So-and-so". We never questioned that we were actually related to these people, although of course none of them were in fact related. They were just aunts and uncles, all over the world, chosen by Mother because she felt they had good ingredients which they might contribute to our "family".'

One 'uncle' in particular, Sidney M. Ehrman, a lawyer who had founded and funded an educational trust for gifted orphans called the Pacific Hebrew Orphan Asylum, provided money to keep the family together on their first expedition to Europe. Indeed, in his autobiography Yehudi says that it was the unhappiness he experienced on his first adventure away from San Francisco, which he had undertaken with only his mother as a companion, that determined Marutha never to repeat this enforced separation from the rest of the family if she could avoid it.

Yehudi's parents had previously decided that he should follow his teacher, Louis Persinger, to New York, where Persinger's quartet was to be based for the winter season 1925–6. Obviously, Moshe could not leave his teaching position for such a long period, but the two sisters, Yehudi and Marutha set out together for the eighty-hour overland train journey. Not that the journey had been made in discomfort. Yehudi and his mother had had their own drawing room on the train, complete with separate lavatory, surroundings which were soon to become all too familiar as touring became 'the family business'.

For Marutha, the return to New York had seemed like a return to hell. The noise and smell of 'a million people scurrying like drowning rats' is an image which has also never left Yehudi. For years, he would cross out the words 'New York' whenever he saw them. 'I always felt that New York *should* have been the leading city in the world,' he told me, 'but that somehow it had missed its chance, or thrown it away.' The nine-year-old boy had lived with his mother near Columbia University on the Upper West Side, close to the Institute of Musical Arts (later the Juilliard School), where he attended musical sight-reading classes. He had only survived six or seven lessons, not because the sight-reading was beyond him; quite the contrary. He had felt 'uncomfortably self-conscious in the anonymity of the classroom', so the lessons were dropped. Although he played occasionally in public, such newspaper reports as appeared were kept away from him. He never knew the extent to which people outside his immediate circle approved or disapproved of his playing. When a rumour reached him that a conductor from Cleveland, Nikolai Sokoloff, had been heard to remark that any of his principal violinists could play as well, Yehudi had been profoundly wounded. Even so, a friend told him, there were not many principal violinists who could play as well as this particular nine-year-old child.

Thus, thanks to Sidney Ehrman, the first journey across the Atlantic, late in 1926, was *en famille*. The nomadic, collective existence was already being mapped out. Moshe was given a year's leave of absence by his San Francisco employers, and the five Menuhins plus numerous violins embarked in New York aboard the French steamer *De Grasse,* bound for France.

Europe seemed part of another planet. The klaxon horns sounded throughout the Paris night, 'the wonders of Baron Haussmann's boulevards' filled the days. Moshe was enthusiasm itself, organizing trips to the Bois de Boulogne, supervising schoolwork, rationing the family's meagre resources. Yehudi recalls a letter he received years later from a lady who had applied for a job as the children's French tutor. Apparently, she had arrived at the Menuhins' apartment on the rue de Sèvres, taken one glance at the three children (eleven, eight and six) sitting at their desks, looking 'oh so serious', and fled.

If anything, the months in Paris reinforced the feeling of Castle

Menuhin. Their apartment was small, the money sufficient but scarce; entertaining not a real possibility. In any case, apart from the musical acquaintances the family met as a result of Yehudi's playing, they didn't know anyone. Yehudi's favourite pastimes, he recalls, were learning history with his father and conjugating verbs with his mother.

Not that he ever felt lonely, he says. 'Above me, I had two elder beings, and below me two younger, a symmetry of love to frame me, the one side matching the other in devotion.' This certainty, this belief in the natural order, this confidence in the world and of his place in it, was the gift of his childhood. It was to prove a gift every ounce as complex and as dangerous as his other gift. He had only been three when, as a result of hearing the concertmaster of the San Francisco Symphony play a solo at the Curran Theatre in downtown San Francisco, he had asked his parents for a special birthday present: a violin.

2

Prodigy

THE VISIT to the Curran Theatre, and the sight of the concertmaster Louis Persinger, had not been Yehudi's earliest musical experience. From the age of two, he had been smuggled into matinee concerts of the San Francisco Symphony by his parents – 'We went to concerts, as we did most things, together.' And only a year later he fell completely in love with Anna Pavlova, both the dancer with her interpretation of 'The Californian Poppy' (a dance to celebrate what was rapidly becoming Yehudi's favourite flower), and her luggage, great stacks of which he discovered one day at the stage entrance of the Curran. 'The image of the travelling artist affected me so deeply that I remember it yet,' he recalled forty years later.

The longed-for birthday gift was also pre-empted by a colleague of Moshe's who had presented the child with a toy fiddle made of metal. Finding he could not make it 'sing', Yehudi had thrown it to the ground and stamped on it. Fortunately, it was not long before Marutha's mother had sent her cheque and a wooden violin been acquired. 'A fiddler in the family?' Marutha said to me. 'That was the last thing we wanted.' But with the great immigration of Russian Jews still a living memory, Yehudi's ambition to be a fiddler can hardly have come as a surprise. Scarcely a family had arrived in America without some member carrying a violin case. It seemed a mere formality that Persinger would accept the boy Menuhin as a pupil.

Persinger turned him down. What need did the concertmaster of the San Francisco Symphony have for a four-year-old beginner? Undeterred, Marutha took her son in May 1921 to the studio of Mr Sigmund Anker ('a drill sergeant'). Progress was agonizingly slow, but every year Anker's pupils were allowed to perform for parents and friends in a private room at the Fairmont Hotel. According to his autobiography, in November 1921 Yehudi played a piece called 'Remembrance'. Although the occasion was not a competition in the strictest sense, the 'prize' for the afternoon was awarded to a twelve-year-old girl. The shock was so great that to this day Yehudi can remember her name, Sarah Kreindler.

Marutha was (and is) nothing if not persistent, and eventually Persinger was persuaded. Marutha tuned the violin, and accompanied Yehudi at the piano for the audition. This time, Persinger accepted. His method was demonstration, rather than instruction. Weekly lessons soon became daily. Although a gentle man, Yehudi told me, Persinger could be fierce, once telling his new pupil to 'go home and not come back until he had figured out the exact rhythms' of a particular piece.

Persinger had studied with the great Belgian virtuoso Eugène Ysaÿe, and later played as concertmaster of the Berlin Philharmonic under Arthur Nikisch. Born in Colorado, the son of a railway signalman, Persinger soon introduced Yehudi to a world of music hitherto beyond his parents' knowledge. Not only to the concertos of Mendelssohn and Beethoven, Mozart and Bach, but also to the musical personalities visiting San Francisco. The composer Ernest Bloch, the Russian Jewish violinist Mischa Elman, and above all the Romanian composer and violinist Georges Enesco. 'He had a great black mane of hair, a lion's mane, crowning one of the most beautiful faces I had ever seen,' Yehudi told me. 'He played the violin with passion and space and virility, and incredible expressiveness. I lost my heart to him then and there, aged six, although it was some years before I came to know him better.'

Yehudi's formal debut was a performance at the Oakland Auditorium midway through a concert being given by the San

Francisco Symphony. He played a duet, the 'Scène de Ballet' by de Beriot; Persinger was at the piano. He was just seven years old. For the next five years, before full-time touring began, Yehudi was only allowed to play in public two or three times a year. But these appearances became increasingly remarkable. A performance at a Christmas concert before an audience of many thousands; a solo later with the Symphony in Lalo's 'Symphonie Espagnol', after which he was described as a 'second Mozart'. Interviews were forbidden; requests to play at private social functions firmly refused.

It soon became Persinger's ambition that Yehudi should study with his own teacher, Ysaÿe. So, after the winter in New York with his mother, and the spring in Paris, *en famille*, plans were finally made to visit Ysaÿe in Brussels. 'We had taken the train [from Paris] the day before, and so come early to Ysaÿe,' Yehudi told me. 'Eventually, the front door was opened by a young lady in a dressing gown! This was quite shocking to me since, although the young lady turned out to be Ysaÿe's wife, I had never seen *any* woman in a dressing gown before, not even my mother. My mother was *always* immaculately dressed, even at the breakfast table. Whatever housework had to be done, she had completed long before we children got up. However, we were taken up the stairs of this bourgeois house to meet Ysaÿe. And there he was, ensconced in an armchair, with only one leg! I had not realized that he had had a leg amputated. So this was my second shock. He asked me to play, and I performed [with my mother] what Persinger and I had prepared, the first movement of Lalo's "Symphonie Espagnol". To my further amazement he began to accompany me by playing pizzicato chords on his own violin! Then, after I had played it – adequately, I thought – he asked me to play a three- or four-octave arpeggio. This I did not do well. And he said: "You should practise those scales and arpeggi, my boy." They were the first words of criticism I had ever had for my violin-playing!

'I fled back to Paris where, by chance, Enesco was giving a concert,' Yehudi added. 'I determined that *he* was my future. After the concert, I stood in line outside his dressing room, not hoping for an autograph, but for his soul. "I want to study with you," I said. "But there must be a mistake, young man," he replied. "I don't give lessons. And in any case, I'm not staying in Paris but leaving early tomorrow morning." "At what time?" I politely enquired. "About seven," he said. "Well, may I *please* come at 6.30?" I offered. He laughed, but my father took me the following morning and I became his pupil then and there.'

Enesco rapidly became Yehudi's spiritual father, a process undoubtedly hastened by Enesco's exotic (albeit familiar) background. The grandson of a priest, Enesco came from Moldavia, so Yehudi convinced himself that he too must have Tartar blood, like Marutha. His name meant 'Son of Aeneas', and his home in Romania was called Villa Luminisch, Villa of Light. His musical intelligence was prodigious; he could play the whole of *Tristan and Isolde* from memory, at an upright piano. One day, Yehudi recalled, he had gone for a lesson with Enesco when Maurice Ravel burst in clutching a new sonata for violin and piano, the ink scarcely dry on the page. Enesco immediately sight-read the whole work, with Ravel at the piano, and then insisted on a second run-through. This time, Enesco played the whole piece from memory.

Enesco, like Persinger, believed in demonstration rather than instruction. 'I played instinctively, uncalculatingly,' Yehudi remembered later; 'neither Enesco nor I gave much thought to theory.' Yehudi appears to have been carried along on a wave of inspiration, and it is astonishing that his technique developed as it did. But it was a high-wire act of dangerous adventure. There was no safety net. After all, a boy of ten could hardly be expected to worry about such things.

The lessons (if such they can be described) continued throughout the winter of 1926-7 whenever Enesco was in Paris, and it was a colleague of Enesco's, Gerard Hekking, who insisted that Paul Paray – an 'important figure in Parisian musical life' – should hear Yehudi play. The result was two orchestral concerts (one including

Tchaikovsky's Violin Concerto) which, because of their 'benevolent reception', signalled to his parents the likely pattern of the future.

A summer interlude with Enesco in Romania – 'the land of legends where gypsies grew out of the earth' and where one of his playmates was the future King Michael – could not divert Marutha and Moshe for long from the decision that would affect their whole life. For Moshe to stay at his teaching post in San Francisco would mean a split in the family. But he knew there was no way Marutha could take all three children on the road, and no way Yehudi could be abandoned. As he liked to tell it, Moshe did not want to leave his teaching post. A nomadic existence had its attractions, especially for one as wild (and Tartar!) as Marutha; Moshe, on the other hand, had travelled enough. From Russia to Palestine, to New York, to San Francisco, to Paris, to Romania. He was a troubled man, and there were dark shadows in his life about which he spoke to no one. The suicide of a favourite sister the night before her wedding; the death of his own father when he was four; both losses which, naturally, he had felt (and continued to feel) profoundly. Moshe instinctively knew that to give up his career in San Francisco would be to abandon his life for the sake of his child. Much though he loved the child, it cannot have been an easy decision. Marutha, on the other hand, had nothing to lose. According to Yaltah, she could not understand Moshe's hesitation, and told him so.

The decision was more or less made for them when a telegram arrived in Romania inviting Yehudi to play in Carnegie Hall with the New York Symphony Orchestra, conducted by Fritz Busch. 'He had wanted me to play Mozart,' Yehudi told me, 'but I insisted on the Beethoven Concerto. "Ah," Busch is supposed to have replied. "One doesn't hire Jackie Coogan to play Hamlet." But as the invitation had come not from Busch but from Walter Damrosch, the promoter, I was adamant. I asked for an audition, and only then was Busch satisfied. The orchestra remained suspicious, and when at the rehearsal I had to ask the concertmaster to tune my violin –

I was not strong enough to twist the tuning pegs myself – I could see their suspicions increase.' That night in New York, 27 November 1927, Yehudi Menuhin stepped into history. Immediately after the concert, however, the eleven-year-old lad was sent off to bed. It was much too late for children to be up and about, Marutha said.

'The concert in Carnegie Hall was actually the second of a pair,' Yehudi told me sixty-two years later, standing on the same stage. 'The first was an afternoon concert at the Mecca Temple, later the headquarters of the Balanchine Ballet, which was then repeated here in Carnegie Hall the following day. I had to come in through the tradesmen's entrance, I remember. And the orchestra's manager, Von Prague, pointed to a big red axe that was by the stage door. It was a fire axe, of course, but I didn't know that. "We use that," Von Prague told me, "for artists who do not play well!"'

Successful though the New York concerts were, Yehudi soon became aware that his repertoire was limited; anyway, he was homesick – for the Chevy. So it was back to San Francisco, and a reunion with Persinger. Persinger had since moved four hundred miles to the south, to Santa Barbara, but once a week during the summer of 1928 he came north with freshly marked copies of the works he thought Yehudi should learn – concertos by Bruch, Glazunov, Vivaldi, Brahms, Mozart and Wieniawski. And it was with Persinger that Yehudi made his first record in the spring of 1928, a ten-inch 78 rpm disc of Achron's 'La Romanesca' and De Monasterio's 'Sierra Morena'.

Plans proceeded meanwhile for Yehudi's first nationwide tour, accompanied in the beginning only by his father, coast to coast, playing once a week for fifteen weeks. But since the whole family was now to be financially dependent on what the concerts earned, a delicate balance had to be struck between the frequency of the concerts and the charge of exploiting a twelve-year-old boy. Thus it was decided to take Persinger along, both as musical mentor and as accompanist. The Shrine Auditorium in Los Angeles; a football stadium in Chicago; Pittsburgh; Minneapolis; and finally back to

New York in the autumn of 1929 where Yehudi and his father stayed with an old family friend, Dr Garbat.

Among Dr Garbat's patients was a Mr Henry Goldman, a noted patron of the arts in New York society. When Goldman discovered that until now Yehudi had only played in public on either borrowed violins or less than full-size instruments, he invited Yehudi to visit him in his Fifth Avenue apartment. Yehudi remembers being amazed by a Cellini bronze, a set of Holbein miniatures and a Van Dyck portrait. Eventually, Goldman just said that Yehudi should choose whatever violin he wanted and he, Goldman, would pay for it. With Persinger's help and that of a violin dealer named Emil Herrman, a 'priceless' Stradivarius was located, the Prince Khevenhüller, so named after the Austro-Hungarian nobleman for whom Stradivarius (by then aged almost ninety) had made it in 1733.

The violin was not, of course, priceless, especially as the Wall Street crash had happened only a few days before, and Goldman wrote out a cheque for $60,000. Goldman had already heard Yehudi play the Tchaikovsky Concerto in Carnegie Hall earlier that year; but now patron and beneficiary were inextricably linked through the Khevenhüller. Goldman became 'Uncle Henry' and was present at all Yehudi's subsequent important concerts. He would sit, with his wife Babette, in the front row, his head inclined towards the powerful yet mellow sound coming from the stage, mature beyond its years, with an understanding almost mystical in its knowledge. Alas, no photographs exist of this extraordinary moment; and probably no photograph could capture what must have gone through old man Goldman's mind. He had heard, although he could not see; Henry Goldman was more or less completely blind.

In the late 1920s and early 1930s, a career (and success) in Germany was essential for any up-and-coming international musician, so the family soon decamped for Europe. After all, most of the concert repertoire then popular was German, or at least middle-European – Brahms, Beethoven, Bach and so on. Fritz Busch, who had conducted the Carnegie Hall debut in 1927, had wanted Yehudi to play with him in Berlin. At the last moment, Busch's father had died and his place been taken by Bruno Walter. So Yehudi's first major European concert duly took place in Berlin on 12 April 1929, just before his thirteenth birthday. Yehudi fondly remembers this momentous event as the 'Mayflower Concert', as in being on board the first Quaker ship to the Americas, since the number of people he has met subsequently who claim to have been there would have filled the concert hall many times over, he says. Fritz Kreisler was certainly there, as was Albert Einstein who, according to Yehudi, came rushing into the dressing room after the concert exclaiming: 'Now I know there is a God in heaven.' Such was the enthusiasm of the audience that the police had to be called to restore order.

The concert 'having replaced Yehudi's barmitzvah', the family journeyed on to Dresden in the south for that promised concert with Fritz Busch. Busch was the General Intendant of the old Semper Opera House, with one of the finest orchestras in Europe (it still is), the Dresden Staatskapelle, at his disposal. 'I couldn't believe the beauty, the comfort, the grandeur, the luxury of what we encountered,' Yehudi told me sixty years later. 'We stayed in the Bellevue Hotel, one of the leading hotels in the world, right on the Elbe, facing a vineyard. Uncle Henry came and gave us lunch. So did Uncle Sidney. Dresden was one of the most beautiful cities in Europe, and with an opera house built by Wagner's architect! I played the Bach D Minor and the Brahms Concertos *before* the interval, followed by the Beethoven Concerto *after* the interval [the same programme as he played in Berlin]. After the concert, at a celebration dinner, I was persuaded to play a little encore, so I performed the Mendelssohn Concerto! And all in one evening.'

'There must have been fifty people at the dinner,' Yehudi told me. 'Fritz Busch made a speech; my father spoke in his half-Yiddish German; I even said a few words. But the highlight of the day, almost, had come during the afternoon when we had all gone to have tea with the Busch family. They had two sons, I remember, and we all played with their electric trains!'

Fritz Busch introduced Yehudi to his brother Adolf, a noted violin teacher, and suggested that Yehudi might benefit from a few months' work with Adolf at his home in Basel, Switzerland. Enesco had earlier also recommended Adolf Busch to Yehudi's attention, so the nomads now moved camp to Basel where life soon took on a recognizable pattern. A secondhand open Packard was acquired, and expeditions were organized all over Switzerland and northern Italy. Marutha discovered an antique shop which supplied her with all manner of Oriental rugs. Tutors were summoned; German lessons began, and Marutha insisted that the children learned to *write* in German as well as speak it. Before long, No. 12 Gartenstrasse, then on the edge of town, became a reincarnation of 1043 Steiner Street. Even the fogs seemed curiously familiar, Yaltah told me.

Adolf Busch was a much more demanding teacher than his predecessors. His attention was constant; 'A student lived with his teacher,' Yehudi remembered, 'making music morning, noon and night.' At first, Busch had insisted that Yehudi did likewise, along with his other pupil at that time, Rudolf Serkin. But, as we have seen, Yehudi had his own family, and anyway Busch had his solo career. With his quartet or as a solo violinist, Busch performed around the world over two hundred times a year, so there was a limit to the amount of time he could devote to Yehudi. Before long, Yehudi was back in the arms of Enesco, back in Paris and what Yehudi himself describes as being his 'first real home' in Ville d'Avray, a suburb of Paris. Soon the Menuhins had their own servants, Bigina the cook and Ferruccio the handyman. Both made superb ice cream, or 'Tra-la-la' as the children called it. They acquired a Delage motorcar, in which Moshe and Ferruccio would descend upon Les Halles early each morning and return for breakfast laden with fruit, vegetables, fresh lobsters and cheeses. Soon the children had learned to bicycle, and been given machines with multiple gears and great balloon tyres.

It would seem that at last the children were being allowed to grow up as children. Until, that is, one considers the 'friends and acquaintances' whom Marutha allowed into the house. Among the guests were the music teacher Nadia Boulanger, the seventy-year-old composer Sir Edward Elgar, the great pianist Alfred Cortot and the eminent Jewish composer Ernest Bloch – a distinguished enough group, but hardly of the same generation as the children. No doubt these elderly musicians were kindness itself, but one can scarcely imagine Alfred Cortot rolling around on the floor or playing hide-and-seek.

Marutha also saw to it that the children had intensive instruction in French language and literature, not by any old teacher who just happened to pass by, but by one of France's most notable authorities on the French language, Félix Bertaux, who was working at the time on what was to become the definitive French–German dictionary. Hephzibah, then aged twelve, was asked to translate a collection of poems by Hölderlin into French. The result (according to Yehudi) gave 'Hephzibah much pleasure'. No doubt it did, but I'll bet she preferred riding her bicycle. If she ever had time, that is, because there were also the Italian lessons, the Russian lessons and the philosophy lessons. A fresh language every summer was the plan. No wonder Yaltah could later say: 'Childhood is such a short time that we should have been allowed to take advantage of it. We never realized the stupidity of many grown-ups, for instance, because [as children] we began to take everything so seriously. Still, at least we can now be children for the rest of our lives; that's what Yehudi told Hephzibah and me. Certainly we never knew, until it was much too late, how utterly isolated we were, that we were not living the life of children at all.'

It has to be admitted that this curious existence did have its compensations, one of the earliest (and subsequently most famous) of which was Yehudi's first musical encounter with Sir Edward Elgar and their recording of Elgar's Violin Concerto. The way Yehudi recounts the story, it has the ring of inevitability about it, as if it were entirely natural that a fifteen-year-old boy should be asked to make the première recording of the violin concerto by one of the best-loved composers of his generation. The concerto contains (for instance) an accompanied cadenza of bewildering profundity, as if the composer were trying to sum up not just the concerto itself, but his whole life's work, indeed his deepest thoughts about his entire life. That Yehudi managed, on the recording, to plumb these depths is breathtaking, especially as his actual technique was then, as now, not always equal to the formidable demands of the music. But on this justly famous recording, it doesn't seem to matter. It is as moving today as it must have been to Elgar at the time, to know (as he told a friend) that his life's work had not been in vain after all.

'It was Fred Gaisberg's idea,' Yehudi told me. 'Gaisberg had been one of the founders of His Master's Voice, and I had already made several recordings for them including the Dvořák and Bruch concertos. I had already been to England in 1929; memories of an open coal fire in the hotel and of the starched white apron of the chambermaid had given me an image of England in which cosiness somehow held grimness at bay. There was a sense of calm security and elegance. The day after my debut at the Albert Hall [in 1929], we had been walking in Hyde Park and an unknown man had come riding his horse along Rotten Row, jumped off, told my mother and me how much he had enjoyed the concert and offered to show us the town. Which he did. He took us to the Tower of London and gave us lunch. And that was the first Englishman I encountered.

'Anyway, Gaisberg was another true "Englishman", and he had wanted to celebrate Elgar's seventy-fifth birthday with the first recording of the great man's Violin Concerto. He thought that I would be "pliant", and thus respond more easily to Elgar's instruction. But I had to admit to Gaisberg that I had never seen the concerto,' Yehudi went on. 'Nonetheless, I mugged it up, in about three weeks I think, came over the Channel from Ville d'Avray, and arrived at the Grosvenor House Hotel, where it had been arranged that I would play the piece through for Sir Edward. I was ushered into his room, where an upright piano and accompanist [Ivor Newton] awaited me. Well, first I had never met a composer who looked like Elgar. Indeed, he didn't look like a composer at all. I was more accustomed to an Old Testament figure like Ernest Bloch. By comparison, Elgar looked like a retired English squire. I began to play, but had hardly got into the first movement when Elgar waved his hands, stopped me and said: "It's such a beautiful day, and I have no worries at all, so I'm off to the races." Whereupon, he left. At the very least, I had been hoping for a few tips. But that was it.

'So we all met again the following Monday morning, 15 July 1932,' Yehudi continued, 'at the studios in No. 3 Abbey Road' (over thirty years later, the Beatles made many of their famous recordings in exactly the same building), 'and there was Sir Edward, imperturbable, courteous and even genial. The orchestra played their heart out for him. I had never seen either such a large orchestra – including trombones and a tuba – or such a cool command over such commitment and dedication from the players. Elgar seemed very pleased with my interpretation because when, later in the year, he and I performed the Concerto in the Albert Hall, he said to me afterwards: "You know, some people have said to me that young Menuhin plays my Violin Concerto too passionately, too intensely. But I *like* it that way. I tell them, that's the way I like it!"' Privately, however, Elgar was wracked with doubt. To Yehudi's father he wrote: 'The attitude of the press, I feel sure, would be that dear Yehudi was making a mistake in appearing with a musician of very inferior calibre (me). I am much too philosophical to feel any hurt at the well-meant slighting of my abilities, but I cannot bear to think of Yehudi being held responsible for anything not of the first rank.'

Almost sixty years later, Yehudi's recollections of his encounter with the bluff, grumpy elder statesman of British music have inevitably mellowed. Other evidence suggests that, by the early 1930s,

Elgar was often embittered and ill-tempered: bitter that what he considered as his proper place in British musical life was now forgotten; ill-tempered because of his increasing deafness and loneliness. The encounter between William Walton and Elgar in a public lavatory during the Three Choirs Festival at Worcester when (according to Walton) the latter was abruptly dismissive of the former's Viola Concerto, has a clearer ring of truth than Yehudi's quasi-sentimental remembrances. Maybe the tall, upright Sir Edward was amused, perhaps intrigued, by this roly-poly young boy from California. He must have been astonished by Yehudi's intuitive grasp of a lifetime of melancholy forever squirming inside a great – but very personal – concerto, even if the (by now) sixteen-year-old couldn't quite get his fingers round *all* the notes. Yehudi's understanding of this tortured music remains in a different league from that of any other living violinist. It is my belief that Yehudi's progress through life has enriched this understanding, but how he could have known what he *now* appears to know when he was only just sixteen remains a mystery, and a miracle.

'When I first met Elgar,' Yehudi told me, 'he seemed the quintessential Englishman. A hunting and shooting type, I felt. And this helped me (I now believe) towards a true insight into his music. In the greatest of musical climaxes, for instance, there was never any brutality, no aggressiveness, no hardness. It was grandeur rather than power. You might even say that the climaxes were benign. In other words, the opposite of the German tradition in which I had been brought up, where a climax meant an all-out assault on the senses; domination through power. That was not my style.

'As we got to know Elgar more intimately – he came to stay with us in Paris in the spring of 1933 – he seemed to us children increasingly like another uncle,' Yehudi went on. 'As none of us had ever known our real grandparents, either on our mother's side or on our father's, Sir Edward filled for us the role of a kindly elderly presence. He suffered from gastric ulcers, I remember, so my mother constantly fed him on onion soup, even for breakfast.

But it soon became clear to me that he was also a deeply mystical man, and that it was this quality which guided his whole being. Inevitably he kept this quality quietly to himself, but once I had appreciated it, I realized that here was the real key to his music. At the time I attributed this feeling to his sense of the past, to a poetic recollection of a world now disintegrating, a world whose values he esteemed and whose passing he regretted. But as the years slipped by, I realized that there was something else: a soulful quality of loneliness beyond anything I had imagined possible, beyond anything I had ever experienced myself.' When one considers, in retrospect, the traumas through which Yehudi's own life was to pass in the twenty years following his meeting with Sir Edward, it is almost as if the Elgar Violin Concerto has become Menuhin's autobiography as well as Elgar's.

Family life at Ville d'Avray, meanwhile, went on. Driving in the family Delage around Paris was 'a superb game'; presumably playing dodgem cars at the Arc de Triomphe was a favourite sport. In his autobiography, Yehudi remembers 'with pleasure' his first sherbet and his first razor. More revealingly, he notes that 'the prospect ... of getting married [was] safely relegated to the future.' Enesco continued to be a dominating influence, urging Yehudi to visit Salzburg and discover Mozart.

Accordingly, Moshe and Yehudi set off in the summer of 1932 for 'operas in the evening' and 'picnics in the mountains during the day'. Mozart's music – according to Enesco – was music of 'syllable and gesture'. I'm not sure if this phrase has any sense at all, but Yehudi interpreted it as meaning music of 'drama', in which every phrase and every note have relevance to some dramatic pattern, an interpretation which (presumably) he hoped would be made plain by 'operas in the evening'. Stravinsky, who believed that music can express nothing, only itself, would have been horrified. But for the teenage Yehudi, music as 'syllable and gesture' seemed pleasing enough.

Family life soon impinged in another way. Hephzibah was now

in her early teens, and rapidly becoming an accomplished pianist. Pierre Monteux, the great Swiss-French conductor, and a regular visitor to Ville d'Avray, noticed that only Yaltah was left out. As for Yehudi, the prospect of having Hephzibah on the concert platform with him was a source of much joy. Her trust in him, he wrote many years later, 'embraced the audience'. 'I felt extraordinarily protective,' he added, 'very much the big brother.' The chaos that eventually was to consume Hephzibah must have come as a terrible sadness for Yehudi, intellectually and emotionally.

Family touring also continued, but was increasingly 'regulated' by Marutha. October to March was for touring; so 'when autumn came,' Yehudi remembered, 'I would sniff it like a colt scenting green fields.' Ironically, although the Menuhins were Americans based in Paris, it was in the United States that the great Menuhin odyssey now began. After trans-shipment to New York, the family hurtled on to New Orleans aboard the *Crescent Limited* train, dining off soft-shelled crab; then to Palm Beach in Florida, visiting the polo fields; then to New York for a confrontation with Toscanini, by then the musical king of America. Marutha did not like him, or his 'peasant origin'. She considered Yehudi had been 'overly humble in [Toscanini's] presence'. Toscanini, she told Yehudi, was petty and ill-tempered.

Gradually, as the American tours began to dominate Yehudi's schedule, Paris ('my first real home') had to be jettisoned in favour of an apartment in the Ansonia Hotel on Upper Broadway in New York. For the first time, Yehudi had serious girlfriends, Rosalie Leventritt and Lydia Perera being the favourites. Yaltah told me that Yehudi fell madly in love with Lydia, the daughter of an Italian banker. Marutha was not amused. Nor was she when Yehudi botched a rehearsal of the Brahms violin concerto and then admitted that he had hurried the last movement because he was late for lunch with a pregnant lady! 'A most sacred condition,' Enesco told him, even though Yehudi was not responsible, 'but your duty to Brahms comes first.'

San Francisco, however, continued to exercise its peculiar fascination; indeed, Yehudi still describes the area around San Francisco as the family's 'Garden of Eden'. Yehudi reminded me that the urge to have contact with the land, 'to plant a tree and watch it grow and bear blossom and fruit', is very powerful in all Jews. It was Biblical and Zionist, and for Yehudi's father this need had 'taken root in California'.

In 1934, the family was invited to spend a summer vacation with friends, George Dennison and Frank Ingerson, at Cathedral Oaks, in the Santa Cruz mountains just outside San Francisco. There, Moshe learned that the adjoining property was for sale. The country-side was wild and untended; cherry trees and apricot trees abounded. The family was elated, and, according to Yehudi, Moshe believed it would be an honour – 'a holy chalice holding all his dreams' – to build a house at the centre of this hundred-acre site, to Marutha's design. Weeks and weeks were spent planning, dreaming, talking about the new home. An architect was hired and thoroughly briefed. The new house, the family's first home they would own since Steiner Street in San Francisco, was to be called Villa Cherkess, after one of Marutha's childhood warrior heroes. The vision of this promised homeland sustained the Menuhins during the long world tour that followed. But the escalating costs of this fantasy eventually caused its postponement. Although Yehudi is careful to point out that the dream never faded, not for the first time (or the last) the real world proved a less certain habitat than his imagination, or that of his sisters. In the event, Villa Cherkess remained for ever a dream; no brick was ever laid, and no Menuhin ever lived there.

Yehudi's first world tour (in 1935) took him to Honolulu, New Zealand, Australia and South Africa, with a farewell visit to Paris and Enesco. Moshe was increasingly anxious to get home, 'sensing Europe's impending collapse'. As for Yehudi, his predominant memory of this year was his discovery that music had form, that a knowledge of the construction of a concerto or a symphony was as important as the technical ability to play all the correct notes. He remembers coming to this realization on a coal-burning liner crossing from Australia to South Africa, the *Nestor*, while watching 'his fellow passengers parading up and down'. Previously he could no more explain *why* he played as he did, than *how* he played as he did. Knowing the structure of a particular concerto might help him towards an understanding of the former, even if he accepted that the latter was probably beyond explanation.

While I have no doubt that this understanding is paramount to any mature musician, it remains odd that, even for a young man as well-travelled as Yehudi now was, the sights and sounds and smells of his first world tour should otherwise have faded from his memory, or at least been replaced by his own particular version of the road to Tarsus. In his autobiography, for instance, he makes no mention of any incident pertaining to Australia or Honolulu, each in their way special, each in their way quite startling when compared with Berlin or Dresden. What was primarily important to him was his own voyage of discovery, about the properness of which he never had any doubts. As one of his brothers-in-law, a Jungian psychologist, was to remark years later: 'Yehudi attempts to make bridges constantly – to people, to ideas, to charitable institutions. He appears to be giving constantly. But I sometimes wonder, especially in the light of the exclusive world in which his mother nurtured him, whether this constant bridge-building is in fact an attempt to discover meaning in things, a pattern in his life, a knowledge which was consistently denied him when young. The danger of any isolation, of course, is that one loses real contact with other human beings, even if, like Yehudi, you are unique and your insights are unique. As a result, the *shadow* for people close to Yehudi has been very great. He is, in this sense, exactly like his mother. He acts in a manner, very convincingly, that *all* of us interest him. But I believe this interest is, for Yehudi, predominantly theoretical. I think the number of people who *actually* interest Yehudi are very, very few indeed.'

This isolation grew following the end of the world tour, not least because of the shattered dream (if, in fact, it was ever shattered) of the home at Villa Cherkess in the Santa Cruz mountains. Yehudi was now twenty, and, as he says, 'the family decided' (note: the *family* decided) that he should take a year off, 'a year of idleness and . . . enjoying ourselves,' Yehudi told me. The family base was to be at Los Gatos, a pleasant suburb about one hour south of San Francisco. (Marutha and Moshe were to live there for the next fifty years.) The house had flowerbeds and an ancient oak, and adjoined a monastery. Yehudi bought his first car, a secondhand open Cadillac V12, complete with whitewall tyres. The family built a swimming pool. Girlfriends came and went – Rosalie Leventritt came all the way from New York, 'a very vital, interesting girl,' Yehudi recalled. Sex, apparently, never crossed his mind. Birthday parties and other celebrations seem to have been frequent; at one fancy-dress affair, Moshe appeared as a coolie. Goats and dogs and ducks were acquired, and each given Crimean names by Marutha; one goat was called Feodosya.

Yehudi didn't touch the violin for months, but clearly pined over Rosalie when she left. In a rare moment of unguarded passion, Yehudi wrote to his favourite confidante, 'Aunt' Willa, bemoaning his loss. She replied with a homily about marriage (again, no mention of sex), which Yehudi kept. 'Fortune has always been good to you, my boy, and I rather suspect her crowning favour will be a girl like [Rosalie]: slight, heroic, delicate, unconquerable.' Then, with unswerving insight, 'Aunt' Willa added: 'Sounds as if I were describing Marutha, doesn't it? Well, like enough you will marry someone much your mother's type.' In October 1937, the 'year off' came to an end, and Yehudi resumed his career and the family its touring. Disaster awaited them, just around the corner.

On the surface, it seemed as if Yehudi's musical life continued much as before, although the rise of Nazi Germany had made touring in continental Europe an impossibility. When the Japanese later bombed Pearl Harbor, however, the need for cultural entertainment in America was transformed. What did not change was Yehudi's continuing involvement with contemporary composers and their work. Indeed, if there is a common thread in all the vacillations of his long career, it is his determination to be involved with music as a living art, as something which is being created here and now, in response to the circumstances of today, by people who are living among us. From Enesco to Elgar, from Benjamin Britten to Dmitri Shostakovich, from Peter Maxwell Davies to Sergei Prokofiev. Most revealing of all, perhaps, was Yehudi's encounter in New York with the exiled Béla Bartók.

Yehudi had decided to include Bartók's Second Violin Concerto in his repertoire, and was booked to perform it in Minneapolis with Dimitri Mitropoulos conducting. The work had only been performed once before in America, and Yehudi was anxious to discuss both the concerto and the composer's First Violin Sonata with Bartók himself. A meeting was arranged in New York (ironi-cally, by the mother of one of Yehudi's girlfriends, Lydia) one gloomy November afternoon in 1943 on the sixth floor of a building on the north side of Park Avenue.

Yehudi arrived with his accompanist Adolph Baller, a Polish Jewish refugee from Nazi Germany whose fingers had earlier been broken by the Gestapo. The two men were shown into a long sitting room, and saw a piano at the far end next to the windows overlooking the street. Bartók was already there, having arrived early in order to position his armchair facing the piano, and also overlooking the street. So the first sight Yehudi had of the sixty-one-year-old Hungarian composer was his back. 'He had the music on his lap, and a pencil, ready, in his hand,' Yehudi told me. 'Just like an old professor, ready to find fault. There was no question of saying "Good day", or, "I'm so happy to see you", "I've really looked forward to playing your work", or "Isn't the weather good?" None of that. As I came to realize, none of these words existed in his vocabulary.

'So I unpacked my violin,' Yehudi continued, 'on a little table at the other end of the room from where he sat, silently. No word. Just tuned and started to play the sonata. I'm glad to say we did play well, and at the end of the first movement he just looked towards me and said: "I didn't expect that a work could be played this beautifully until long after the composer was dead." Those were the very first words he said. He then smiled, sat down, and we continued.

'Well, you can imagine what that meant,' Yehudi said. 'Every bit of ice had been melted, and I began to see that all of Bartók's passions, his worries, frustrations, ecstasy, his rage, tenderness – everything, was in his music. Looking at this frail old man sitting overlooking Central Park, however, you would never have guessed what lay within him. He seemed like a transparent parchment. Very pale, very thin, gaunt, incredibly tense. But his eyes were glowing embers. They seemed to penetrate everything. There were no secrets for those eyes. What's more, you couldn't lie to Bartók, emotionally or factually. It would have been quite impossible. And it was not just his incredible erudition, his knowledge of Latin and Greek. It was his understanding of the winds, of geology and of the ways of animals. He was like a Red Indian in the field. You felt that every inch of his being was alive to everything about him.

'I was desperate of course to commission something from the great man,' Yehudi continued. 'I began to feel that our relationship was such that I could have asked him for an opera! But that would have been an imposition, too greedy on my part. I knew that he needed commissions to support himself in exile, although the idea that he was left high and dry when he arrived in New York and died of starvation is absolutely absurd. ASCAP, the American Society of Composers and Publishers, for instance, had offered Bartók a great deal of help, even sending him on holiday to Alabama! The Boston Philharmonic had commissioned the Concerto for Orchestra; Benny Goodman had wanted a piece; Columbia University had given him a job.

'No, the difficulty was that Bartók was an impossible man to help,' Yehudi explained. 'He would accept no sympathy at all. You just couldn't put your arm around him and say: "Oh, poor man, how sad it must be for you to be in exile!" It was the last thing you felt you could say to this solitary, awesome figure. So, eventually, I summoned enough courage to ask him for a solo sonata for violin, and I immediately sent him a cheque for a thousand dollars, a substantial sum in those days. A year later, the work arrived, in my view perhaps the greatest work for solo violin since Bach. And do you know, he never cashed the cheque until well after he had finished the work and delivered it. Such was the integrity of the man.

'Bartók posted me the score from Asheville, North Carolina,' Yehudi explained, 'from a hospital where he had been sent by his doctor in a last desperate attempt to find a cure for his leukaemia. We had invited him to our home in Los Gatos to recuperate from whatever surgery was thought necessary. But he could no longer travel, he said, and instead wrote to me: "I am rather worried about the *playability* of some of the double-stopped [passages]." Indeed, I had had exactly the same worry. "I should like your advice," Bartók went on, "so I enclose two copies. Would you be so kind as to introduce in one of them the necessary changes in bowing, and perhaps the absolutely necessary fingering and other suggestions, and return it to me?" In fact,' Yehudi told me, 'I eventually suggested very little, finding what Bartók had written difficult, but possible. We met again just before I gave the first performance of the Sonata in the Carnegie Hall. Maybe I had persuaded myself by now that such was the spirit of cooperation between us, that I could ask him for one minor change. Just one simple chord, which, if simplified, would make one whole passage more negotiable. So I asked him. He looked at me for what seemed an age, although it was probably no more than a few moments, transfixing me with that unforgettable gaze. And then he just said, "No."'

'It was a wonderful performance,' Bartók wrote to a friend a few days later. 'I was afraid it [the Sonata] was too long; imagine: listen [sic] to a single violin during twenty minutes. But it was quite all right, at least for me!' 'Nine months later he was dead,' Yehudi told me, 'although his body had to wait for another forty years before it could be returned to his beloved Hungary.' 'That I should have provoked this magnificent music,' Yehudi wrote later in his auto-biography, 'is a source of infinite satisfaction to me; that I should have played it to Bartók before he died, remains one of the greatest milestones of my life.'

I have included at length the story of Yehudi's encounter with Bartók, because it seems to me characteristic of all that is noble about Menuhin. And in the chaos that was to come, I think it worth remind-ing ourselves of what is undeniably great about the man. There will be some discussion later about his true status as a musician. About the man, moreover, there is abundant (and growing) evidence to cast doubt on the familiar image of the saintly Buddha of the violin world to which we have become accustomed. During his early years as a prodigy, it is clear that life for Yehudi was a game, at which the whole Menuhin family undoubtedly became skilful players. The darker side of his life has been, if not unknown, at least uncharted. He appears to have had no curiosity, for instance, about those things which obsess most adolescents – sex, violence, his place in the world, his relationships with others. Or if he had such curiosity, he either suppressed it, then or later, or else he never admitted it, to others or to himself. His non-relationship with Rosalie Leventritt is always expressed in the cool terms of a man not wanting to admit he had sexual passions like any other: 'a vital, interesting girl' is not how most adolescents would describe the awakening of sexual feelings. And there cannot be many eighteen-year-olds who simply decide to take a year off in 'idleness, just enjoying ourselves'. After all, it's not as if his life until then had been such an enormous struggle that he was pausing for breath before the next great leap forward. As Zamira, Yehudi's only daughter, told me, 'My father was never allowed to cross a street by himself. Every time he had a cold – and this continued until he was well into his twenties and married – one of his parents would insist on rubbing his chest or his back and provide all the medicines and inhalations he needed. It wasn't so much that there was no fresh air in the household. Whatever air there was, came from another planet.'

At the same time, the generosity and humility with which Yehudi approached Bartók shines through any amount of back rubs or days of 'idleness' spent 'building a swimming pool'. The childlike pleasure (Yehudi was actually twenty-seven) in being able to satisfy this grand old man of music (Yehudi describes Bartók as 'the greatest composer of our century') is very moving. Equally, there is no doubt from his correspondence that Bartók was also greatly moved by the young American violinist's intuitive understanding of a world of sound that must have been completely alien. In one particular passage in the last movement of the Solo Sonata, for instance, Bartók had written a whole series of quarter-tones, a sound more usually associated with Indian or Japanese music and which should have been, therefore, mysterious to a young man fed and watered on Beethoven and Brahms. And although Yehudi later simplified this passage in his edited and published edition of the Sonata, it is a musical tribute to him that at the time he attempted to overcome this complex writing.

In later years, Yehudi's mastery of the equally wayward yet magisterial Violin Concerto by Alban Berg remains the inspiration for many contemporary violinists, even though, once again, Yehudi often seems unable to play all the right notes. It's almost as if he had abandoned mere technique in favour of some greater understanding, way beyond simple familiarity with the notes themselves. Musical history is peopled with performers whose initiative has been responsible in part for the birth of many great works. But there is something profoundly touching about Yehudi's uncomplicated belief that this has been his mission in life. As a prodigy, he has had many equals among performers, although not perhaps among violinists. But as a man who has in many ways remained a child prodigy throughout his life, he has no equal among those who have sought to bind up the wounds of creativity through patient and continuous sponsorship.

The long sad decline of Enesco, for instance, and Yehudi's unselfish devotion to his former master, is little known but again nearer to the man than many of his better publicized charitable works. Enesco had married a princess of Romania, whose previous husband had ill-treated her and left her 'wretched'. After the Second World War, very little of the princess's property remained, having been either destroyed by the Germans or confiscated by the Soviets. Exiled in Paris, the Princess Cantacuzène had gradually been forced to sell off what little furniture remained to keep body and soul together. Enesco was her one joy, and had become a sort of court musician who entertained her ever-declining circle of friends. The problem was that by now Enesco was himself increasingly crippled by a wasting disease of the spine. He could hardly stand, and soon was almost permanently bent double. And this was the man whom Yehudi had described as the epitome of all a composer should be: the shock of black hair; dashing; vigorous. Now he was reduced to a pathetic dwarf, a condition made worse (for Yehudi) because Enesco chose to live with his princess in the same apartment in Paris to which Yehudi had first come for lessons almost twenty years earlier.

While Yehudi was in Paris – and he went there especially to visit Enesco – he visited him daily; he gave concerts to try and raise money for him; he took safe keeping of Enesco's Guarnerius violin, in case the Communists demanded its return as state property; later, he received as a gift Enesco's own first violin, a Santo Serafino, acquired while Enesco was still a student playing in Vienna, and with which he had once played for Brahms. And when Enesco eventually died (in 1955), Yehudi campaigned relentlessly to found an Enesco Museum in Bucharest, as well as a conservatoire in Paris in Enesco's name. Today, the Enesco Museum in Bucharest flourishes, with manuscripts, scores, letters, photographs and other memorabilia. There is a state violin competition, the Concours Enesco; there is also an Enesco Conservatory of Music. And in the establishment of all these institutions, Yehudi – acknowledged by now as a world figure – played an indispensable role.

Similarly in memory of Bartók. In Hungary and Budapest, which Yehudi visited soon after the end of the war, Yehudi insisted that his concerts of Bartók's music were relayed by loudspeakers in the squares and streets outside the concert hall. More controversially, Yehudi's championship of German musicians (performers *and* orchestras) who had stayed in Nazi Germany and were, therefore, thought to have been collaborators and so could find no employment after 1945 is again witness to Yehudi's understanding of the human predicament. His relationship with the great German conductor Wilhelm Furtwängler, despised after 1945 as being the 'Nazi conductor', is a long and troublesome story to which we shall return later. Suffice to say here that the relationship raised the hackles of zealous Jews everywhere, and made a visit to the new state of Israel virtually impossible for some years. Even as late as 1957, when Yehudi insisted on playing the Bloch Violin Concerto with the New York Philharmonic as a tribute to that 'Old Testament prophet' of his childhood, who was by now neglected and dying, the taunt of anti-Semitism still hung in the air as a result of Yehudi's supposed 'collaboration' with ex-Nazis.

So, while it would be quite wrong to accuse Yehudi here of naïvety in the ways of the world, his simple honesty is often interpreted in that way. 'The problem is,' his second wife told me, 'that Yehudi hasn't got a wall to back against. He was not taught to believe in evil, so he doesn't. Which is nice for him, but not so easy for the rest who have to keep the evil away from him. It's not easy living with someone who never suspects, who never believes that people may be asking for favours with ulterior motives. Anybody can push him, and he just disappears into the distance.

'From the beginning, his parents taught him to follow a distant light. So he doesn't want shadows or motes to get in the way,' she told me. 'Or if they do, he simply shuts his eyes and goes into a dive.' And so, following this distant light, the young Yehudi began to concern himself with events beyond family, beyond day-to-day relationships, events that were – in his eldest son's words – 'cosmic in scope'. It was not simply that he had been cosseted and protected from an early age from the normal buffets of the storm; it was not that he was unaware of the sufferings to which all human beings are subjected; it was not that he was incapable of reaching out to touch another human being in pity or in love. It was more that he never doubted the clarity of his vision, his distant light. He had come to believe that to all things there was an inevitability, a sense of justice, of virtue and of goodness.

The discovery that this was not so, and that the world held no such promise, no such assurance, knocked him completely off the rails.

3

Marriage

Nᴏʟᴀ Rᴜʙʏ Nɪᴄʜᴏʟᴀs was a busty, bouncy Australian from Melbourne. Her father was Cornish and her mother Scottish. They had emigrated after the First World War when Australia had seemed a land of plentiful opportunity. Zamira, her daughter by Yehudi, told me that Nola was 'emancipated'. She had auburn hair, drove a white Jaguar motorcar 'with panache', played tennis, swam and generally 'larked about'. She was not beautiful in a classical way, according to Zamira, but her hazel eyes and the assurance with which she carried her buxom figure made it clear to all who met her that she knew about men. When she first met Yehudi backstage at a concert being given by the Melbourne Symphony Orchestra at London's Royal Albert Hall, she was just nineteen.

The twenty-one-year-old Yehudi was completely 'bowled over' (his own description), and overnight the two became almost inseparable. Two weeks later, a concert engagement took Yehudi to Holland, and there, on his first night away, he locked himself in his room, telephoned Nola in London – 'muffling my voice as best I could beneath the pillows' – and proposed marriage. Nola 'was understandably startled'. She hardly knew him, she said. 'Ah,' replied Yehudi, 'I hardly knew Persinger before "electing him" to be my teacher; and I hardly knew about the violin before deciding that was to be my life.' Upon his return to London, Yehudi quickly won Nola over, and on 26 May 1938 they were married, in Caxton Hall, London, 'by a British civil servant'. The ceremony was held one day earlier than originally planned, Yehudi reminded me, 'so that we might not miss a performance of the Verdi Requiem by Toscanini'. It was less than two months since the pair had first met.

The home movies taken during their honeymoon in Yosemite Park show a young couple brimming with love. She constantly petting and kissing him; he, chubby and still a boy in some ways, giggling inanely at the pleasure of it all; she, 'larking about' in her nightclothes, fondling a dog, an irrepressible bundle of energy and happiness; he, paddling in a stream, a little embarrassed by the relentless attention, trying to give as good as he's getting. It is romantic, delightful and clearly fun, and it is easy to see why her daughter, Zamira, insists that 'everyone loved Nola'. Everyone, according to Yehudi, including Marutha. 'She welcomed Nola as a new daughter,' Yehudi told me, 'full of good will and the wish to please.' Maybe (Yehudi speculates) Marutha saw in Nola a truly kindred spirit. After all, Marutha's father had abandoned her mother before Marutha could have known him, and Nola's mother had died when she was only seven. 'I imagine,' says Yehudi, 'that [Nola] found in our close family unity an intriguing warmth.'

In fact, according to Yaltah, in the spring of 1938 Yehudi was wildly in love with another girl (Rosalie Leventritt?), 'but my mother didn't think this other girl would be a suitable mother for her grandchildren. So she found this charming, healthy girl called Nola, and decided she would be more appropriate. It was all a game of chess for Mother, probably because her own marriage was so meaningless. I believe my mother could have lived with anyone, under any circumstances, and still have made destiny her own. After all, she always described Moshe to me in terms of "I picked a very good father for you."'

It's worth remembering (and repeating) that there are those in the family who believe that Yaltah's complaints have a tired and predictable quality about them; that she is not therefore the most reliable of witnesses; and that it is quite wrong of her to suggest that Yehudi's was an 'arranged marriage'. There is no doubt that he wanted to marry Nola, and there is no doubt that each partner was much in love with the other. Even Yaltah admits that Yehudi was 'not just married off without love'. But she also recalls, for instance, 'an extraordinary moment' on the boat returning to America after the wedding. This was to be our last crossing together as a family, since both my sister and I were also shortly to be married. The whole family would walk around the deck as usual, but my mother demanded that Nola walked one or two paces behind, just to make sure that she was constantly reminded of her proper place. Yehudi, for his part, considered Nola as a new sister, someone who was going to do all the things his sisters did, and maybe one or two things they didn't [sic]. So this poor, beautiful girl, Nola, suddenly had to *want* to study, *want* to learn poetry, *want* to look up in dictionaries every last word, and pretty soon she didn't have any-thing spontaneous left inside her that wasn't criticized. And all this happened in five days on the boat. We saw the indoctrination taking place, like a spider getting hold of this lovely victim, this unsuspecting, trusting soul. It was horrible to see.'

This is not a view which Yehudi accepts. Indeed, he finds Yaltah's whole approach to their mother and childhood distorted. 'Yaltah and my mother didn't see eye to eye. She feels that she suffered at my mother's hands and that of course creates resentment. But in fact my mother is one of the most remarkable and wonderful women in the world, selfless to a degree, having given herself completely to her children, and a woman of great pride, integrity, of absolute honesty, a strong and wonderful woman.'

Yet, according to Krov, Yehudi and Nola's only son, 'Marutha insisted on controlling Yehudi's married life to an unbelievable extent. I've seen many of the letters my grandmother wrote my mother soon after the marriage. [My grandmother] would write to my mother in German, knowing full well that Nola could speak no German. So my mother had to try and learn German in order to please, not Yehudi, but my grandmother. The letters are full of detailed advice: when to abstain from sex, what foods she must feed him on, how she must behave towards him in public. No doubt my grandmother was acting from the best possible motives, but I think it must have made Nola's life fairly difficult.' Yehudi, however, sees Krov's recollections as part of an idealization of Nola's role in his life. Krov's belief that his relationship with Nola was 'the one glowing period of my life is inexcusable.'

'It was like seeing what had happened to us,' Yaltah goes on, 'only condensed. I mean, at least we were Marutha's flesh and blood. But to do that to someone outside the family, who didn't *have* to go through it, was a terrible mistake.' 'Marutha felt that Nola needed a mother,' Zamira added, 'and she tried to mother her in much the same way as she had mothered her own two daughters, Hephzibah and Yaltah. I'm sure my grandmother would have found fault in her daughter-in-law whoever she had been. But she deliberately tried to mould her into an acceptable daughter-in-law who could, for example, recite Heine at the drop of a pin. To the end, long after the marriage had been lost, Nola, my mother, could recite one particular poem of Heine: "Du bist wie eine Blume . . .”!'

'Nola played a great part in all our lives,' Yaltah reminded me. 'She was our first bridge to youth, because she was a real young woman.' It was as if a huge gust of wind was blowing away the family cobwebs (or at least attempting to do so). Nola had an elder brother, Lindsay, as handsome and dashing as Nola was extrovert and girlish. Hephzibah was 'completely smitten', according to Yehudi. Undaunted by the prospect of life in the Australian outback (Lindsay was a sheep farmer) – or, possibly, relieved at the chance of getting as far away as possible from Marutha – Hephzibah announced her engagement only days after that of Yehudi and Nola, and the two were married under an oak tree in Los Gatos six weeks after Yehudi and Nola had set the pattern in Caxton Hall.

And then, even before Hephzibah was married, Yaltah, the youngest, apparently despondent at the thought of being abandoned by her brother and sister, frightened at the threat of being locked in the closet again (if only figuratively), announced that she too was getting married, 'to a man she hardly knew and certainly didn't love'. William Stix was an honourable, charming Jew from a respectable business family in St Louis, whom Yaltah had met briefly while the family had been in Paris the previous year. Yaltah was not yet sixteen.

'Our parents,' Yehudi said later, 'gave us a mass benediction.' They also left each child with an appalling burden. 'A letter my sister should have had,' Yaltah told me, 'from someone she loved very dearly, while she was making up her mind about Lindsay, rather mysteriously never got to her and her destiny was changed. We never found out until months later, by which time it was too late.' And lest one should think that it was only Marutha who was involved, one should not forget Moshe's obsession about the suicide of his favourite sister, the children's only real aunt. 'Every so often,' Yaltah told me, 'I'd have marvellous conversations with my father. And I remember him telling me one day about the sister he loved very dearly who had killed herself. It seems that she too had been sent a letter from another man, who was her real true love, the night before her intended marriage to someone else. Believing that her true love had forsaken her – the letter having been intercepted by an older sister who was really like a mother to her – and not being able to face a loveless marriage, she had poisoned herself. And my father's eyes were so full of pain when he told me this. And he'd tell it like a secret, so that no one else should be let in on the burden he felt he was carrying. He said that, if only he had known, he could have saved her. And when did he choose to tell me this? In 1938, when I was about to be married to a man he knew I didn't love.'

Nola and Yehudi, or to be more precise Yehudi, had given little thought as to where they would live after they were married. 'Clearly,' Yehudi writes in his autobiography, 'my parents were not going to thrust me out of their house,' which seems a rather odd way of expressing the desire on Yehudi's part for setting up house and home with his new bride. It appears not to have occurred to Yehudi (or his parents) that the newlyweds might actually *want* to live in a place all their own, until Nola's father turned up at Hephzibah's wedding and told Yehudi a few home truths about married life. Rather shamefacedly, Yehudi moved into a worker's cottage that had been the only completed part of the Villa Cherkess dream estate, and called it 'Alma', 'after the railroad station at the bottom of our land'. Still, they thought at least it wasn't named after some never-seen village in the Crimea. Sadly, Nola soon felt its uncomfortable isolation to be almost as remote; worst of all, it was later realized that there *was* a Crimean river called the Alma. No ocean, no horses, no tennis court; only the squirrels and the avocado trees. Ah well, says Yehudi, 'my parents accepted this development serenely, as though it were perfectly natural for a married son to leave his parents.'

Thinking back on the honeymoon home movies, and in the reasonably certain knowledge that Yehudi was inexperienced in every sense when he married, it is clear that the physical excitement of being with such an obviously passionate woman bounced Yehudi along the tricky path of early marriage. Like any first real sexual encounter, it must have utterly transformed the man, and opened for him an infinite number of emotional as well as physical doors, almost simultaneously. When one considers the lengths to which his parents had gone to protect Yehudi from any part of the world which might impinge on his talent, it is a miracle that Yehudi's brain was not completely scrambled by the excess of new and radically different information which it now had to absorb. Indeed, it is rather touching that, almost forty years later, he still cannot find a satisfactory language with which to describe this period. In his autobiography he writes of 'crossing the unmarked boundary that separates the men from the boys'. He knew 'no accommodation for [his] desire other than eternal vows'. The marriage was 'an enterprise', 'an extraordinary adventure', a 'growth', while fatherhood (when it came shortly thereafter) 'gave this growth a useful

impetus' [sic]. Yehudi followed Nola's first pregnancy 'with philosophical attention'.

Even allowing for the rapid change in sexual attitudes during the
last decades, it is difficult not to laugh at these mawkish statements.
I am not questioning for one moment that this is exactly *what*
Yehudi felt, and exactly *how* Yehudi would have expressed his
feelings to Nola, to his mother or in a newspaper interview about
his marriage (which he did). Maybe if Nola had been raised in a
convent, in the Middle Ages or in a strict Catholic country, then
she might have understood what Yehudi was talking about. But
you sense that she (and her brother) might have come straight off
Bondi Beach. She knew men, was not afraid of sex. Life was for
living. She was unsophisticated, vulgar (by Marutha's standard) and
fun. That was her attraction, and that is why Yehudi loved her. 'I'd
given her such complete assent,' he told me. 'I realized then that she
had been raised in a more modern way than I, and I realize now
that I had approached our marriage with a preconceived notion of
duty, of seriousness. What I did *not* realize until years later was that,
at the time of our marriage, I was scarcely out of the kindergarten
in which my parents had brought me up. I can see now that I was
not "emancipated" in the way that Nola was. I was certainly not a
saint; nor did I imagine that I had married a saint. But I did imagine,
and believe, that the relationship into which I had freely entered,
was going to be on the highest possible level, and was going to be
for ever.'

Their first child, a daughter, Zamira, was born ten months after
their marriage. The name means 'songbird' in Hebrew; in Russian,
'Zamir' is 'for peace'. Their second child, a son, Krov, was
born a year later. Krov is partly an invented name, although in
Russian (with only minor changes in pronunciation) it can mean
'blood' or 'shelter', as in roof. Krov's earliest memories of his
father are of walks in the country and picnics. What he appears to
have forgotten is that lunch on these picnics often consisted of
raw brains and fresh cows' milk. As to Nola, so overjoyed did

Yehudi become at the prospect and accomplished fact of father-hood that 'he would have taught Nola the innocence of Eden!', although how he proposed to do this is unclear. Nothing had prepared him, he admitted to me years later, for 'the sound of a voice which had never been heard before'. And as soon as Krov was conceived, Yehudi proposed that the whole family – pregnant wife and tiny child – should go on tour with him. After all, was this not what families did?

By chance, the first foreign tour they undertook together was to Australia. (Indeed, Krov was born in Melbourne.) Yehudi had been there before, with another family in tow, but in describing his return visit – among other things, to his sister Hephzibah and her new husband, Nola's brother, Lindsay – Yehudi uses a curious phrase. The return to Australia with Nola, he says, was 'the first time the country [had] penetrated my flesh'.

Hephzibah and Yehudi gave concerts together, in Melbourne and Sydney, with Nola somewhat resolutely sitting in the higher balconies, 'hoping by that expedient to make me play to the gallery', Yehudi told me. But Nola wanted more from Yehudi than merely having him play to the gallery. Although he certainly became increasingly dependent on her – in fact probably transferred his dependence on his mother to dependence on his wife – she also became increasingly besotted with him.

What had begun simply as love had now become for her a wild passion, almost as if this were the only way she could repeatedly demonstrate her love for him. She could not compete with him intellectually; she could not compete with him culturally – she remained to the end, like many wives of great musicians, com-paratively ignorant of the finer nuances of her husband's art, and was not ashamed to say so. But she could arouse in Yehudi an emotional fury that hitherto had been denied him, and which (more importantly) hitherto he had denied himself.

'Marutha had prepared, she hoped, a perfect man,' Krov told me. 'But she had forgotten, at the same time, that he was a human being;

forgotten that he was a man like any other man, who would respond to a woman like any other red-blooded male. And Nola seems to have understood this; she was right. There was no way, given his upbringing, that Yehudi could resist. For the first time in his life, he was fulfilled, emotionally, physically and therefore professionally. Nola added a whole new dimension to his life, and when, eventually, she left him, that state of fulfilment, that sense of family, disappeared from Yehudi's life. Or maybe he just shut it out from his life, like turning off a cold water tap. Either way, I don't believe he has ever found such happiness again. I don't know whether he has even looked for it again.'

It was perhaps unfortunate that the beginnings of the marriage with Nola coincided with the onset of the Second World War. Although, being an American citizen, the exigencies of war did not directly affect Yehudi until the Japanese bombing of Pearl Harbor on 7 December 1941, his knowledge of and nostalgia for a Europe now engulfed in flames worried him greatly. Dresden, Berlin, Paris, the cities of his youth, were now closed to him and, as far as he could see, being systematically vandalized. Only London had thus far escaped, but there seemed little guarantee that London's freedom could survive for much longer. All this was quite apart from the rumours and press reports of Jewish persecution now beginning to reach America, not all of which, it was thought, could be without foundation.

Nonetheless, the touring continued, at least to those parts of the globe where it was still considered safe to travel. And it was maybe with safety in mind that Yehudi persuaded Nola to stay behind in California. Thus, two tours of South America were undertaken alone, and he was on his way to Mexico with his by now regular accompanist, Adolph Baller, when the Japanese attacked. The story of Yehudi's selfless efforts during the subsequent war must wait until later. As far as Nola was concerned, it meant simply that her man was gone. It would obviously have been difficult, if not impossible, for Nola and two small children to accompany Yehudi on the countless missions which he now flew, courtesy of the American Air Force, to entertain the troops. 'More effectively even than marriage,' Yehudi recalled later, 'war cut me adrift from the past.'

This is not to say that, within the limits of his schedule and also of his understanding, he did not attempt to be a dutiful father. At least, for a time. Among Krov's memories of his father at this time are presents of chocolates, smuggled back from some exotic location in Honolulu; and of Yehudi insisting that the family collect eggs, although only Yehudi had the courage to sit there and eat them fresh and raw.

'My mother quite naturally wanted a closeness, a proximity, to my father,' Krov told me. 'From being the centre of a social whirl in Australia, she had almost overnight been transformed into a lonely wife on a hillside in northern California.' Paradoxically, she had been taken out of a very parochial environment into a world which must have seemed cosmic by comparison, but from which, through nobody's fault, she was now being excluded. She also lacked the experience, or perhaps the willingness, to build bridges to Yehudi's parents who, although only a few miles away, seem to have done little to help her through this difficult time.

Yehudi tried. That is clear. Whenever he could, he took his two children to his concerts in America. Zamira remembers vividly the first performance of the Bartók Solo Sonata in Carnegie Hall, when she was six. 'I sat in a box, all dressed up,' she told me, 'with my brother asleep on the floor. I leant over and was transfixed by seeing my father on the stage and also by the music he was playing. Later, when the marriage had collapsed and I was living with my mother, missing my father dreadfully of course, I clung to a recording of the Bartók Second Violin Concerto, and learned it all by heart, to keep alive that memory of Carnegie Hall. Of course I missed him as things began to go wrong,' Zamira told me. 'But if you're privileged to have such a father, you have to share. You can't have everything, can you?'

But Nola *had* wanted everything, and who could blame her? Finding she had less than she needed, she began to drink. She now convinced herself that, in fact, she and Yehudi had little in common, and told him so. Yehudi claims she gave him the news even before Krov was born. 'Obviously, the words themselves struck me very strongly,' Yehudi told me, 'mostly because I just wasn't ready for an *independent* life. I was a *dependent* male; so, if anything, Nola forced me into a true realization of exactly how dependent I was. Alas, I never took any of the strong-arm methods which one is supposed to, which are supposed to be the right thing to do in these circumstances.' What circumstances? Had Nola taken a lover? 'When the possibility first struck me,' Yehudi told me, 'I was totally dumbfounded. Instead of looking upon the situation as an inevitable development, of saying, ah well, if I'm free then she is free, I couldn't bring myself to accept what was happening. Maybe it was cowardice. Maybe it was a complete lack of reality on my part. Maybe I just couldn't throw to one side something that had been so fresh in my life.'

'Yehudi often used to ring me up and say: "Just think, I've got my two sisters and my very own wife,"' Yaltah told me. 'It was just like: "See my toys. See what I've got for Christmas." Certainly he was made to look down on sex by his father, which is probably the only way in which my father could live with my mother, by saying, oh well, sex is unimportant. Never mind. She has other qualities. After all, for Yehudi it was the violin which was everything. But you can control a violin. You are responsible for what it sings, because it's your violin. A girl, however, is someone else, although Yehudi believed he was well prepared for the encounter. When we were just adolescents, for example, we were invited to a wedding where we knew there would be dancing. Yehudi was so concerned that he took lessons – not in dancing, he was already quite a good dancer – but in when and where he should put his arm round a girl, his dancing partner; when he was allowed to look at the girl; when to hold her arm or her hand, and so on. He took everything so seriously. But I don't think he ever held a girl in his arms the way he held his violin.'

When Nola persuaded herself that Yehudi was also being unfaithful (an inevitable by-product of his increasingly peripatetic existence in what he himself describes as 'masculine free-and-easiness'?), her drinking increased and with it the moral opprobrium of Marutha. To this day, Marutha has no photographs, as far as I know, of her first daughter-in-law (certainly, none are on display in Marutha's home), never mentions her name, never even admits (at least, not to outsiders) the existence of 'a first wife'.

For her part, it is clear that Nola could no longer accept the idea that family life – especially when married to a wandering violinist – had any meaning at all without the physical closeness she craved. As a consequence, the marriage drifted. Yehudi seemed paralysed. Unaccustomed to failure, he had no idea how to deal with it, and so didn't. Nola found consolation where she could, realizing (I believe) much earlier than Yehudi that their marriage had been an illusion, at first full of happiness and light, but an illusion nonetheless. Being tougher both by temperament and upbringing, she convinced herself the marriage could not continue, and so she dumped him.

Such confidence as she had, Krov told me, in herself, in her marriage, was being sapped by Marutha, by her loneliness, and by her *own* feeling of failure. So was it Nola who actually took the decision to end the marriage? 'I have never blamed Nola,' Yaltah told me. 'Nor did Hephzibah. Because we loved her so greatly. She was what we would have liked to have been. And whatever he says now, at the time Yehudi suffered for years because of the failure of his marriage. I never asked him, but I remember to this day how he looked. I wish I *could* have asked him: "Is there anything I can do?" But I couldn't. You see, in our family we never talked about these things because, in our family, we didn't feel. Or at least, we were not supposed to. But how can a family go through such things and not be in touch with their own, true feelings? Yehudi was heartbroken; the children were being taken away from him, and he adored his children. And he adored Nola. Because that was *the* wife; that was his wife.'

To this day, Yehudi finds it difficult to face up to what happened. In his autobiography, Nola is not even properly listed under Menuhin, Nola, but under Nicholas, Nola, and then occupies less than ten pages out of three hundred and ninety-three. All he would say to me of his feelings about his first wife was that, 'as an unsophisticated, inexperienced young man, I can see now that the motives got confused. One could love something [sic!] which appeared to be so refreshing and so new and so bright, that one was naturally taken in. Not by the person, I mean, but by the situation. I'd never been disillusioned before, and so I did not expect to be so now. I felt certain that I could not take the first step to end the marriage.'

Who knows the exact chronology of events in the break-up of any relationship? But it does seem that Nola initiated the collapse. Bored with her life in California, tired of the constant haranguing she got from her mother-in-law, disappointed that Yehudi could not understand what she wanted from their marriage, alarmed by the painful discovery that a violin virtuoso is not necessarily a good husband, Nola had simply taken a lover. Perhaps this new relationship was meaningless, as it often is in such circumstances. Perhaps Nola was becoming more and more suspicious of Yehudi's 'life on the road'. Even Yehudi admitted to me that one of the few sensible pieces of advice he'd ever been given was that 'any misdemeanours should always be with married women.' And Diana Gould, whom he had begun to see in London as early as 1944, was not a married woman.

But if it was Nola who had physically taken the first step, it was Yehudi who was the more devastated. As we shall see, he attempted to find some consolation in a frenzied schedule of entertaining US troops. More importantly, as Yaltah points out, he tried to hide in the one world he felt he knew, music. 'When everything goes wrong in your life,' Yaltah told me, 'the first thing you try and do is go back to what you imagine to be the *security* of music. But you can't *use* music in this way; you can only serve it. You cannot, for instance, use it to mend a broken heart. Yehudi should have taken time off, just gone to look at the sea and lick his wounds. But he didn't; he chose to go on, with his tent. These halls, the concerts, the empty chatter. "Mr Menuhin, what do you think of this or that?" He left himself no time to re-establish himself, spiritually or emotionally. He was trying to live *in public*, while suffering.'

'It was also very hard for someone like Yehudi, who had grown accustomed to a structure in his life which was quite independent of his feelings,' Yaltah continued. 'Suddenly his feelings had become so overwhelming that they impinged on the structure and the structure disintegrated. And then what are you left with? Eventually, your health is threatened; and for a violinist, when your health is threatened, so is your violin-playing. And if you try to pretend there is *nothing* wrong, when you simply try to suppress all these feelings, you go crazy, you get sick and you die.

'Yehudi was supposed to be above these things,' Yaltah told me. 'He believed he was above all these things. He thought he could endure it. And no friend close to him had the courage to recognize, at this time, a man who was suffering like any other because he had been rejected. He was blaming himself. He felt guilty. He was frightened and lonely, and no one helped him, not even and especially not his parents.'

The divorce was not finalized until the summer of 1947, the grounds being Yehudi's adultery. As Yehudi describes it, Nola 'refused to divorce me'. It appears that the problem was much more concerned with what grounds were to be given for the divorce. In his autobiography, Yehudi does not mention them. Some years later, Hephzibah wrote Yehudi a stunning letter which is remarkably perspicacious about Yehudi's divorce. The worst thing about us, she wrote, is 'our lack of contact with life as it is generally lived among those who were not absolutely sheltered from every day's troubles, as we were. It made awful fools of us.' Most extraordinary of all, she admits that 'other people had never entered our lives before as definite factors'. Work had been 'holy'; life, as most people know it, irrelevant. 'We were helpless,' Hephzibah wrote, 'in coping with the conflict between what we had been taught and what we were being taught.' Later: 'In spite of nursing the world's finest intentions, we have done more harm to people we loved than we ever believed ourselves capable of doing to people we didn't love.'

According to Krov, once Nola had made the decision to leave Yehudi – it was, after all, the only real possibility open to her – the damage which she suspected Yehudi and his parents had done to her became all too apparent. 'What little confidence she had left in life,' Krov told me, 'was shattered. One must not forget that she had been plucked out of a local environment in Australia, where she was queen, into marriage with a world-famous musician. She had needed help, and Yehudi had not provided it. Marutha had undermined Nola's faith in herself, and now she was left with nothing.' Krov told me that his mother never said anything against Yehudi to her dying day, and always sought other channels for the bitterness she felt about her failed marriage. After Yehudi, she was soon to marry again, to an English ex-RAF pilot; according to Krov, he did his best in an impossible situation. But he was a weak man, and he too had a drinking problem which only exacerbated (according to Krov) Nola's increasing dependence. So she divorced again, and married again, to a man 'vastly inferior to her'. The drinking got worse, and many of Krov's early adolescent memories are of fetching his mother in and out of various clinics and hospitals. 'I remember when I was only fourteen,' Krov told me, 'I had to fly her from Geneva to Paris to put her in the American hospital in Neuilly' (Yehudi claims that this was at Diana's insistence and his own expense), 'because she was incapable of doing it herself.'

'What the two of them should have done,' Yehudi's second wife – referring to Yehudi and Nola – told me, 'was have a roaring affair which would have done him the world of good, and would not have done her any harm. They had nothing in common,' she added, 'and that was that. What went wrong with the marriage was that she was disastrously wrong. Her drinking became intolerable; her profligacy, both sexual and material, legendary. When I met Yehudi, he was practically bankrupt!'

After the separation, Yehudi never refers to Nola again in his autobiography. In none of his published books does he mention her death (in 1978); nor the funeral which his two eldest children attended. He includes only one photograph of her; indeed, I do not believe he possesses more than one or two in the whole of his extensive photographic archive. Nola has been simply blotted out of his life. Or at least, it looks as if that has been the intention, although according to someone present he broke down and wept when told that Nola had died, blaming himself for her descent into alcoholism. Like all great love affairs, Yehudi's first marriage was never to leave him.

4

War

W AR WAS the second shock Yehudi had to endure. Not the
fact of war, although that was brutal enough, but what happened to him as a result of his particular involvement in the war
effort.

In describing his activities during the war years, Yehudi (in his
autobiography) makes an odd admission. 'Normally,' he writes, 'the
artist is *impersonal* to the extent that he is not expected to *engage* his
audience by any means other than music' (my italics). The admission
is surprising because if ever there was an artist who had benefited
from his image, both as child prodigy and later as saintly inspiration,
it is Yehudi. And it is hard to believe that he is unaware of this,
unaware that he *is* engaging his audience by means 'other than
music', engaging his audience in reality through the power of his
personality. He admits that before the war he had never had to play
in 'cafés, cabarets or ... brothels' [sic]; in other words, it appears
he had never felt the need to *please* his audience. In which case
his decision to play for the US troops during the Second World
War was either a moment of utter folly, or else the inevitable consequence of his crumbling marriage, because here was an audience he
would *need* to please, would *need* to engage by means 'other than
music'.

He claims that he was exempted from US military service until
the final days of the war merely because he was 'the father of two
children', which is self-evidently untrue, although what he actually

did was probably far more valuable to the military than carrying a gun. His experiences at the front and in the remoter camps inhabited by US troops, however, finally broke asunder the cocoon that Marutha had so painstakingly woven, and which Nola had already begun to tear apart. They drew him inexorably into the world of affairs and the world of other men. He also claims that no matter how traumatic these experiences became, his inner ear, his musical instinct, never deserted him. But there are those who maintain that *after* the war, Yehudi's violin-playing was never as rich, never as beautiful as it had been before. It would seem that the world, like his sexuality, rose up and punched him in the face.

It is impossible to calculate how many concerts Yehudi gave between January 1942 and July 1945. Before the war, he gave on average no more than sixty concerts or recitals per year. In the years of the war he gave over a thousand. Even Yehudi admits there were 'hundreds' – in Alaska, in the Aleutian Islands, in Puerto Rico, in Shemya, criss-crossing the Atlantic in RAF bombers, playing in aid of the Free French and de Gaulle at the Royal Albert Hall, in Brussels while the Battle of Arnhem was being fought two hundred kilometres to the north, in Antwerp at a hotel only just vacated by the Gestapo, and, finally, in Belsen only a week or so after it had been liberated. On this last occasion, his accompanist was Benjamin Britten. Peter Pears told me years later that it was a moment of such horror that Britten would never talk about it, even to his lover; except one night, when Britten told Pears that what he and Yehudi had seen had left such a wound that no piece of music he had subsequently written was untouched by the memory. For Yehudi, as we shall see, the event was equally devastating.

One does not know what the battle-weary GIs made of Yehudi. 'In this tender, passive, softened mood,' Yehudi remembered, 'the most unexpected people [were] sensitive to the most unexpected music.' What is certain, however, is that Yehudi suddenly met a whole world of people with whom he can have had no direct contact before – 'some conversation had to be made with the wounded in the wards', is a somewhat unlikely description of barrack-room banter.

Not that I am doubting the complete sincerity with which Yehudi threw himself into his task, but it's odd that once again, over thirty years later (when he wrote those words), Yehudi still lacked the appropriate language with which to describe his experiences. And these were surely real enough; a recital in the far north of America when the piano keys froze solid, forcing him to play unaccompanied Bach; a concert in Honolulu for marines about to throw themselves at the Japanese guns – they were like men who 'moved as ghosts under a burden of unhappiness and dread'; and then a second concert a few days later for most of those same marines, or what was left of them, 'bruised, bloodied and bandaged'. 'The endless lines of ambulances . . . three shows [sic!] a day.' And this was the boy who had sat in the back of his limousine only a few years earlier watching ordinary people coming and going, as if in a dream, their activities like 'ants in an anthill', altogether 'preposterous'.

In some ways, war for Yehudi was little more than a big lark. With his accompanist, Adolph Baller, he certainly got into some scrapes. Outside lavatories that were blown away in a storm with the unfortunate Baller squatting inside; hiring horses in Phoenix, Arizona, because there was simply no other form of transport – 'two less convincing cowboys [it would have been] hard to find'; the endless jabs against typhoid, yellow fever, dysentery, malaria, cholera and diarrhoea. And all this quite apart from the unpredictability of wartime air travel, strapped into metal-frame seats, bumped from one island to the next, aborted landings, botched takeoffs – one plane finished up in a sugar cane field, on its nose; 'excursions' (Yehudi's description) over enemy territory, lost in fog when, luckily, the Japanese were unaware of their distinguished visitor.

Although Yehudi will happily admit to these Boy's-Own excitements, his innate modesty refuses (even now) to allow him the full realization of the amazing work he did. For the American public, most of those who 'entertained the troops' became, quite properly, national heroes – Bob Hope, Bing Crosby and Betty Grable, for instance, who together probably did more for the American war effort than a ton of Eisenhower speeches. In Britain, popular entertainers were just as active, although it was the contribution of classical 'entertainers' which, for some perverse reason, caught the 'popular' imagination; Dame Myra Hess, sitting lumpenly in the National Gallery playing Beethoven's 'Moonlight' Sonata, is a key image of London prevailing under the Blitz. Yehudi, on the other hand, being by this time neither truly American nor truly European, failed to capture the public imagination on either side of the Atlantic; his efforts during the war, accordingly, have been largely overlooked. But it is clear that he did as much as, if not more than, any other classical musician of his time. His commitment was total, his enthusiasm endless, and his stamina beyond belief. Few other practising musicians can have used their twenties (Yehudi was twenty-five when the United States declared war on the Japanese) to better purpose.

It was not simply the rough and tumble of life with the troops, although that must have been unusual enough. Nor was it the attempt to drown the sorrow he felt over his broken marriage in work, work and more work. Nor was it even the realization that there was more to music than the edification of the soul; music, as Yehudi's sometime accompanist Benjamin Britten remarked later in his famous lecture at the Aspen Music Festival, must be useful, and to the living. The war made Yehudi a man – emotionally, sexually and intellectually.

He soon found himself at the centre of political and social controversies, a position he has occupied – albeit reluctantly – ever since. This transmogrification took on unforeseen dimensions later, but its origins are in the war years. It is hard to imagine, for instance, the chubby young man who had charmed Elgar and who had astonished the musical capitals of Europe, as a union man. But a union man he became, and with a determination that it is tempting to describe as militant. To take only one example: the American Guild of Musical Artists had been founded by Yehudi's fellow violinist, Jascha Heifetz. It was not the first musicians' union in the United States, however, this being the American Federation of Musicians, whose boss in the early war years was an autocratic trumpet player, Claudio Petrillo. The principal purpose of the AF of M was to offer protection for salaried musicians – such as members of orchestras, dance bands and session players. As such, it did not affect Yehudi and his membership had not been sought. But Heifetz now wanted to extend union membership to include all *solo* artists, and so had founded his own union. Heifetz had written to Yehudi inviting him to join, giving as a reason the likelihood of European solo artists flooding the United States after the war, thus threatening the livelihood of those whose country it was – an irony, since Heifetz was himself an immigrant. 'We Americans must stick together in self-defence,' is how Yehudi remembers Heifetz had put it to him.

Yehudi declined – what did he know about unions? – but he could not escape the battle that was soon joined between the rival organizations. In fact, many solo artists *had* rallied to Heifetz's call, and he now began to enrol those orchestral members (previously with the AF of M) who had aspirations for a solo career. Not surprisingly, this angered the AF of M. Petrillo realized that Yehudi was still a free agent, and argued that there could be no better recruit to their ranks than one of the most famous of all solo artists. It would be a public snub for the Heifetz union, as well as a useful bonus in the AF of M's increasing struggles against the burgeoning greed of the record industry. After all, was not Yehudi a star of the record industry as well?

Yehudi acknowledged that he was vulnerable in so far as most of the orchestral musicians he was likely to play with in concert would be members of the AF of M. What if they were to boycott him? His recitals for the troops would not, could not, last for ever. So when the invitation to join the AF of M came from Petrillo, Yehudi decided to stall as long as he could. What exactly were the laws, by-laws and regulations of the union to which, as a member, he would have to freely submit? he enquired. Yehudi now claims he was offered bribes to become a member; in fact, Petrillo let it be known that an unusually high fee would be offered for a certain concert in Chicago (where else?) if Yehudi would declare his membership. Eventually, the Philadelphia Orchestra refused to play with Menuhin as soloist, and Yehudi realized he had no choice. He joined the local branch in San Francisco.

But he had been sufficiently bruised by the experience that he soon awoke to the many injustices against which the union, however hamfistedly, was fighting. It was true that the recording industry (as always) took a disproportionately high percentage of the profits of any high-selling record. Yehudi suffered from this as much as anyone. It was also true that many employers – the all-powerful radio stations being the worst culprits – hired and fired without any consideration for the well-being of those who were hired or fired. Yehudi soon found himself championing the cause of Toscanini, for example. After years of service at NBC Radio, including the establishment of one of the finest of all American orchestras, the American Symphony, Toscanini now found himself, in his late seventies, on the scrap heap. The advent of television had apparently made the idea of a Radio Symphony Orchestra redundant. But America's loss was Italy's gain. In the post-war years, Toscanini returned to Italy, and lived long enough (in Milan) to foster the talent of another messed-up American, Maria Callas.

Although Yehudi eventually found himself powerless to help Toscanini directly, this ill-treatment of a great conductor left an abiding impression. It strengthened his determination a few years later, for instance, to help another conductor in trouble, Wilhelm Furtwängler. The true story of Furtwängler's relations with the Nazi Party will probably never be known, although there is enough film of Furtwängler conducting the Berlin Philharmonic – with Hitler and his gang sitting in the audience – to condemn Furtwängler forever in the popular imagination. The fact that, in the 1930s, Furtwängler had frequently provoked Nazi wrath by supporting fellow musicians in trouble was conveniently forgotten. The composer Paul Hindemith, among many others, had much cause to be grateful to Furtwängler. Although not Jewish himself, Hindemith had a half-Jewish wife and resolutely gave work in his orchestral and chamber concerts to Jewish musicians. Worse, he had written an entire opera – *Mathis der Maler* – as a coded attack on the Nazis, as a result of which Hindemith's entire works had been banned in the Third Reich. Furtwängler had ignored this ban, and promptly performed the symphony extracted from the opera. He had only managed one performance, but it was a rather more courageous act than the grubby little telegram sent to Goebbels by Richard Strauss, congratulating the Nazis on banning the music of Hindemith and thus 'weeding out undesirable elements in German cultural life'.

In post-war Germany, under Allied occupation, Furtwängler, like thousands of others such as Winifried Wagner, had had to undergo de-Nazification. Furtwängler became at best a non-person, despite the considerable evidence in his favour at the tribunal. He had refused, for instance, to accompany the Berlin Philharmonic on propaganda visits to the occupied territories; he had frequently invited soloists who were Jewish (including Yehudi) to appear with the Berlin Philharmonic in Nazi Germany before the war (not surprisingly, they had all refused, although the invitations had certainly existed); he had even confronted (and angered) Hitler, as Winifried Wagner's daughter, Friedelind, later recalled. When Furtwängler had objected to becoming a tool of Nazi propaganda, Hitler had threatened him with a spell in a concentration camp. 'In that case,' replied Furtwängler, 'I shall be in very good company.' According to Friedelind, Hitler was so taken aback that, instead of losing his temper, he hung his head and walked away.

None of this, of course, was known to the general public; not that it would have made a scrap of difference had it been known.

In post-war America, the only good German was a dead one. So when Yehudi returned from Europe to New York late in 1945 and was asked at a press conference his present view of German culture, he volunteered the information that, of all the musicians who had seen it as their duty to stay in Nazi Germany, the one who commanded most respect (and thus would be most welcome in the United States) was Wilhelm Furtwängler.

The outraged foaming at the mouth of American Jewry as a result of Yehudi's casual remark was bewildering. Admittedly, Western consciousness after the ending of a bloody war was still so prickly that for a Jew (Yehudi) to be seen supporting not only Hitler's favoured conductor, but also by implication Hitler's official court orchestra, was too much to stomach. For a man who had been brought up to believe that music was holy, its ultimate purpose spiritual, philosophical and healing, and its practitioners essentially different from ordinary mortals, the uproar was a shock. As we have seen, the effects of Nola leaving him had been damaging enough; but Yehudi had attempted to push that experience aside by blaming himself, or at least to diminish it by persuading himself it was of no more than passing interest. As we have also seen, his war experiences with the troops had begun to open his eyes and his mind to the existence of other mortals not like himself. And while I am sure that playing for Marines about to be shot to pieces by the Japanese was a heartrending moment never to be underestimated, Yehudi does tend to remember the war years in part as a continuity of those crazy days of his childhood when outings in the open-topped Chevrolet along the dusty roads of Yosemite Park were all a big adventure.

But Yehudi was a Jew, *the* Jew. His name proclaimed it. And here he was, through his support of Furtwängler and the Berlin Philharmonic, suddenly confronting the Holocaust and its aftermath. It is hard to believe that he ever expected a fair hearing; but again, is this not what his childhood had taught him? Justice for all men, regardless of class, race or religion? 'We were mentally cognizant of every problem,' Hephzibah wrote, 'but only as a *theoretical* dilemma.' 'Like everything else in our family,' remembered Yaltah, 'we never realized until it was too late that the world was not as we had been led to believe. And so we have had to constantly resurrect ourselves like corpses, but now with half our brains gone and our hearts pickled.'

In 1945, something in Yehudi had told him enough was enough. Nola; the AF of M; maybe the sight of the exiled Bartók in 1943; the terrible awareness that a world of suffering existed towards which, like any artist, he was being inexorably pulled. Yehudi felt he had no choice, and rose up to protest against the injustice done to Furtwängler. He insisted on going to Berlin to play with 'Hitler's orchestra', the Berlin Philharmonic; indeed he was the first non-German soloist to do so after the war, let alone the first Jewish soloist. It was an act of solidarity for which the Berlin Philharmonic has remained profoundly grateful ever since. When I asked permission to film Yehudi with the Berlin Philharmonic, I expected a polite refusal or else a fee so massive that *any* filming would have been impossible. (Under von Karajan, the Berlin Philharmonic became a notoriously greedy orchestra.) To my amazement, the reply from Berlin was immediate and positive. Anything that Yehudi wanted, they told me, was acceptable to them and, what's more, they would accept no fee.

Although the first concert after the war (including the Brahms Concerto) was conducted not by Furtwängler but by Sergio Celibidache, there is little doubt that Yehudi's presence helped re-establish the Berlin Philharmonic's respectability. Within a year, Furtwängler himself was reinstated.

In America, meanwhile, the Chicago Symphony had invited Furtwängler for a series of concerts. Contracts were exchanged and plans made, whereupon the Jewish lobby in Chicago – important, since they were the orchestra's principal sponsors – announced a boycott. Incensed, Yehudi announced what he called a 'counter-boycott' and refused to play with the Chicago Symphony for many years. Furtwängler was to repay Yehudi manyfold, by providing (for instance) the orchestral accompaniment to what is perhaps the greatest of all Yehudi's recordings, the Beethoven Violin Concerto. Indeed, it is one of the finest of all recordings of the Concerto, and so closely did the two men's lives become intertwined that Furtwängler was later a witness at the marriage of Yehudi's sister-in-law to the Hungarian pianist Louis Kentner.

The price of this friendship was great, however. Yehudi was publicly branded a traitor and a collaborator. Some of his concerts in occupied Germany were boycotted, even some of those he gave in displaced persons' camps. At one free concert, for example, only five people turned up. One newspaper announced that it would follow Yehudi 'like a curse until your conscience awakes', and compared his playing with those Jewish orchestras who had been forced to play for concentration camp inmates while they were being gassed or hung. Wherever he went, Yehudi was booed and hissed and shouted at. In Central and South America, an entire tour was threatened. The Jewish mafia, which controlled musical life in New York, was equally hostile. No further invitations came from Carnegie Hall or from the Symphony Hall in San Francisco. And when the state of Israel was founded in 1948, Yehudi waited in vain for two years before a visit could be arranged, and only then in the face of a threatened assassination attempt. His first concert was given under armed guard. Even Yehudi's father, Moshe, caught the backlash. Although he died of cancer, Marutha still blames the Zionist lobby for what she believes was his comparatively early death.

As a result of these setbacks, Yehudi now seems to have become possessed of an almost missionary zeal. He began to criss-cross the lunar landscape of Europe in much the same way as he had criss-crossed America in the 1930s, except that this time the travel arrangements were rather more primitive. In Romania he raised a fortune for the Red Cross and for various Jewish charities – Bucharest had become the unofficial Jewish capital of Europe in the years between the end of the war and the foundation of Israel, and there were over two hundred thousand Jewish refugees in Bucharest at this time. In Czechoslovakia, he played Dvořák's Violin Concerto in Prague for the Russian military authorities; on a second visit, he was arrested as an agent provocateur and confined to prison, believing he was about to be sent to Siberia.

And he was also the first Western soloist to get to Moscow, where his naïve enthusiasm became so great that eventually it clouded his judgement. Greeted by the great Russian violinist David Oistrakh, fêted at official banquets as if he had single-handedly engineered the Russian–American pact which had brought down the Nazi regime, eyed suspiciously by Dmitri Shostakovich, Yehudi sailed through Moscow like a conquering hero. He stayed at the Metropole Hotel, overlooking Red Square, renowned then as now for its caviar and sturgeon. Indeed, so swept away was he by Russian hospitality, that the manifest cruelties of the Russian regime seem to have escaped him. In his autobiography, Yehudi writes of meeting the father of the exiled Russian cellist, Piatigorsky, in the foyer of a government building. 'This cursed regime,' the old man cried out. 'It doesn't care for its old people. It leaves them to rot. It has no heart, no pity.'

The full horror inflicted by Stalin on the Russian people was, at that time, largely unknown. But the particular treatment of certain individuals (and musical colleagues) such as Shostakovich was suspected even if not fully realized. *Pravda*, after all, was available in the West, and it was *Pravda* which had denounced Shostakovich's music in 1937 as 'negative, grinding and meaningless'. Oistrakh later gave Yehudi a facsimile copy of Shostakovich's First Violin Concerto, although the origins of the concerto seem to have been of little interest to him; he prefers to describe this tormented work as simply providing the violinist with 'gratifying opportunities to bring the house down'. In fact, the concerto was written in a white heat following yet another public denunciation (as a result of which Shostakovich thought he was going to be shot), and then hidden to

avoid further disgrace. Is it conceivable that Oistrakh (to whom the
work is dedicated and to whom the manuscript had been eventually
entrusted lest the authorities tear it up as they had done the manuscript of Shostakovich's Ninth Symphony) can have made no
mention of the circumstances in which the work was written? And
considering the number of times the two violinists played together
in later years, is it possible that Oistrakh never talked about one
of the most important instrumental compositions of recent years?
Oistrakh was, by all reports, a prudent and careful man, as well as
a supremely gifted violinist. But he would never have tolerated
Yehudi's view that, had Shostakovich been 'free', the composer
would have been 'more experimental' and repudiated the 'blatant
effects' that 'coarsen his best writing'. If ever there was a composer
who spoke directly to us of his condition and of his times, it is
Shostakovich. Did Yehudi not notice this, or did he prefer not to
notice? Did his missionary zeal in fact have limits, or had his mind
already moved on to other things?

'Without a doubt this was the worst period of my life,' he later
admitted. 'How far had I fallen from my childhood dream of
universal peace and harmony.' More importantly, he had also begun
to accept that, ultimately, there were also limits to music's ability
to heal. He began to describe the mistakes he felt he had made in
his private life as 'crimes', as he 'drifted nearer to disaster than at
any other time'. Yehudi now speaks of this 'miserable period of his
life' as a result of his indecision (and that of Nola) in putting a final
end to their marriage. Certainly this must have been a factor, but I
believe it was a symptom rather than the cause.

In the summer of 1945, and again in the autumn, and again in
1946, he undertook a series of visits to recently liberated concentration camps – now euphemistically described as Displaced
Persons Camps – which had a profound effect. They would have
done so on any man or woman, but for a Jew, the son of Marutha
and Moshe, the child prodigy for whom even shopping for food
was a 'preposterous' activity to be avoided for ever, they were a

cataclysmic shock. The most important of these visits was probably the first, to Belsen, with Benjamin Britten as accompanist. Britten, the conscientious objector, the homosexual, the fugitive, the outcast whose opera *Peter Grimes* had rewritten English musical history only a month before; and Menuhin the Jew. Their pilgrimage, for such it was, just as Marlow had journeyed to find the heart of darkness, was the strangest voyage in all of Yehudi's long life.

'We *wanted* to play there,' Yehudi told me eventually. I had been dreading asking him about his memories, knowing as I did about Britten's reactions through Peter Pears. It is some measure of the trauma Yehudi endured that, over forty-five years later, he could only speak about Belsen haltingly, groping for words, and then crying at the memory. 'We were shown the actual remains of ... people' (even that word caused him trouble), 'and where the bodies had been gassed and burned. And all that remained were ... gold teeth, which the Nazis had intended to melt down.

'Of course, no one had then seen the films of Belsen or Auschwitz,' Yehudi went on. 'We knew a little of what to expect, but nothing could have prepared us, psychologically or visually, for what we found. Such things only existed for me in fairy tales. The sounds and cries of agony in the German hospitals we visited, while the ghastly tortures lived on in the imagination of the survivors. There was one little child, a gypsy boy aged about four. His parents had been killed, but he was one of the most engaging and beautiful little children I'd ever seen. I would have loved to adopt him, but I suddenly felt I had nothing to offer him. I never found out what happened to him. I realized also that, if *I* had been caught by the Nazis, I would probably have not been able to control my temper. I would have been like everybody else, full of revenge. Whether that vengeful feeling would have lasted, I do not know. I have met survivors who are no longer vengeful. Admittedly they are a minority but, nonetheless, having suffered the most unspeakable tortures, having seen their families being destroyed, they cling to the idea that they too are human and might, under certain circumstances, have behaved in exactly the same way as the Nazis.

'What I had also underestimated,' Yehudi told me, 'was the extent to which these survivors were waiting to hear music! Decades later, I still receive letters from all over the world from people who remember our coming to Belsen and what it meant to them, dressed in their army blankets, haggard, gaunt faces, without hope.' Britten and Menuhin gave over thirty concerts in and around Belsen, often in old SS barracks, 'trying to impress on our minds an actuality beyond imagination'. It was not until years later that Yehudi was able to put this nightmare into some perspective. 'The measure of a civilization,' he told me, 'is how long it is able to prevent turning people into brutes. The Japanese stabbing women and children as they plundered their way through Manchuria; the massacres of Genghis Khan; Jewish soldiers shooting Arab children in the occupied territories; the list is endless ...' Again his voice tails away, as if his mind can no longer cope with the horror of it all.

After all, nor could Kurtz as he 'cried in a whisper at some image, at some vision – he cried out twice, a cry that was no more than a breath – "The horror! The horror!"' Joseph Conrad's hero and the frightful journey he took could almost have been written about the journey Yehudi had made from his childhood in San Francisco to this awesome moment in Belsen. But, unlike the fictional Kurtz, there was no messenger from the darkness to call out, 'Mistah Kurtz – he dead.' Yehudi still lived, but the shadow of Belsen was for ever cast across his path.

'After Belsen,' Yaltah told me, 'Yehudi was never the same again. What man would have been? The effect of Nola leaving him, added to what he saw in Belsen, almost destroyed him.' It is my belief that the frantic activity of the immediate post-war years (the 'missionary zeal') was in part panic, desperately trying to escape from the mess he had made of his life and what he perceived as the chaos around him. Like Kurtz, Yehudi knew that the horror he had seen 'had the appalling face of a glimpsed truth – the strange commingling of desire and hate'.

But if the horror transformed the man, it also knocked the violinist right off balance. And this was a man whose life, indeed the only life he knew, was as a violinist. He was running. He was afraid. And he was not yet thirty years old.

5

Humpty-Dumpty

THE SCENE: the Russian Tea Room in New York, next door to
Carnegie Hall where Yehudi had made his formal New York debut
over sixty years earlier. Lunchtime, and Sir Yehudi Menuhin, Order
of Merit, Croix de Guerre, nominee for the Nobel Peace Prize,
Member of the Académie Française, Knight of the Realm, is talking
with Lady Menuhin, Diana Gould as was, ballet dancer for Diaghilev, keeper of the purse and mother of Gerard and Jeremy, slightly
older than Yehudi, a feisty, indefatigable, autocratic, witty 'fiddler's
moll' (her description). They are trying to explain to me how and
where they first met.

YM: 'It was 1943, I think.'
DM: 'Oh no, it wasn't.'
YM: 'Well, it was either in 1942 or 1943.'
DM: 'No, no, no. It must have been much later.'
YM: 'No, no, it was well before the end of the war.'
DM: 'I know it was later because I was acting with Michael Red-
grave at the time. I was, in fact, *with* Michael Redgrave, so it
must have been 1945.'
YM: 'No, it couldn't have, because I clearly remember it was long
before the end of the war.'
DM: 'That's right. The war was finished in France, but not in
England.'
YM: 'But it wasn't finished in 1943.'

73

DM: 'It was in 1944, darling. I'm talking about 1944.'

YM: 'That's right, but the meeting *I'm* describing was in 1943!'

DM: 'It was 1944! Oh, Lord in heaven above! Will everybody bear witness to this! Yehudi always knows *best*, but *I* know the facts! And he knows best because he can pull the truth in all directions. It was 1944. September the 29th, and *I* say so. Have I got home at last?'

YM: 'Oh, well.' (Yehudi sniffs apologetically.)

DM (quick as a flash): 'Do you want a handkerchief?'

YM: 'Thank you, darling. But I *do* remember our wedding. We tried to do it in secret at the Chelsea Registry Office, with only the immediate family present. There was just time for a quick glass of champagne, before I had to rush off to a rehearsal.' (To me he says:) 'It was all rather unfair to Diana in retrospect, because it was, after all, her first marriage. And after *my* first, rather over-publicized, wedding, I didn't feel like making another lot of noise for something real.'

DM: 'Oh, so *that* was it.'

YM: 'Yes.'

DM: 'So now I know, forty years on.'

YM: 'Not forty, surely?'

DM: 'Forty years on, come October 19th.'

YM: 'Ah yes, but I meant that that was ...'

DM: 'I'm not saying that it's now forty years since ... I'm talking about myself, get it? All the photographs, by the way, look as if I had nabbed him, which didn't add to the joy.'

YM (desperately trying to change the subject): 'Well, violinists do hold a certain attraction for women, I think.'

DM: 'Oh, why?'

YM: 'Oh, I'm quite sure of it. I think it's very much like ...'

DM: 'Like tennis, you mean.'

YM: 'Yes, yes. Like tennis. Standing alone on a stage, giving yourself to your inspiration.'

DM: 'So *that's* why I married him. Now I know! I've been wondering about it for forty years, saying to myself, "Now what *was* it?" And now I know!'

Yehudi and Diana collapse in fits of giggles, to the apparent annoyance of our fellow diners. A private game between two old friends, no doubt, played out with relentless energy for my benefit. A knockabout, quick-fire repartee, worthy of Nichols and May.

There is much reason to believe that Diana Gould rescued Yehudi Menuhin from the suicidal course into which his life was apparently tumbling at the end of the war. Depressed, almost bankrupt (according to Diana) as a result of Nola's extravagance, aware that something had gone seriously wrong with his violin-playing, Yehudi must have presented a sorry sight.

There is also little doubt that Diana has encouraged (some would say invented) the saintly image that now bestrides the world, an image which has partly obscured his increasingly insecure violin-playing. She was probably the first to realize that, breathtaking though his violin-playing had been and would still occasionally be in the years to come, this was paradoxically the least interesting aspect of the man. Or if not the least interesting, it was in the end an aspect which was flawed and possibly could not survive on its own. After all, we do not remember Albert Schweitzer either because he was a great organist (he was not), or because he was a great mathematician (he was not), but for his muddled and outdated attempts to help lepers in central Africa. Similarly, we do not remember Galileo either because of his inventions (mostly copied), or his astronomy (in detail often wrong), but for the great moral and philosophical stand he took against the secular and religious authorities of his time.

Menuhin has claims to be in that company, although (as we shall see) I believe the social mores of the late twentieth century have ultimately prevented him from making a lasting contribution in the manner of a Schweitzer or a Galileo. But that, finally, has become his claim to importance and lasting value: not just as a violinist (who, except violinists, can remember the great instrumentalists of fifty years ago?), but as a humanitarian of dignity, wisdom and goodness. And it was Diana Gould who first grasped this nettle. As she told me, her task has been to 'set about putting Humpty-Dumpty back together again. He had fallen,' she added, 'from a very great height. Worse, he did not know why.'

They might have met when Yehudi was only eleven. The two friends from Los Gatos – George Dennison and Frank Ingerson – had told the Menuhins about a remarkable family they had met in London, two girls and a boy, and a mother who was a famous musician. They had nearly met again in 1929 when Yehudi passed through London to make the acquaintance of some distant relatives, Uncle Jack and Aunt Edie, who lived in Richmond. (Aunt Edie, it turned out, also knew the Gould family.) But, notwithstanding the merry banter above, Yehudi and Diana in fact finally met in September 1944 at the Belgravia apartment of Diana's mother, Lady Harcourt, again at the prompting of Messrs Dennison and Ingerson. According to Diana, Yehudi telephoned her mother to announce that he was in London. Although Lady Harcourt would certainly have known who Yehudi was, she was not the kind of person to take such an unsolicited call lightly.

'Oh really,' Lady Harcourt replied. 'And what do you want?'

There was a long silence, broken eventually by Lady Harcourt who said: 'Well, speak up. Who are you and what do you want? Lunch or dinner?'

'Oh well . . .' mumbled Yehudi inconsequentially.

'It's only rations,' warned Lady Harcourt, 'but I suppose you'd better come round.'

So round he went, to lunch, with Diana, her sister Griselda, Anthony Asquith (the film producer and founder of the British Film Union) and Lady Harcourt. 'We were all very grey, very crumpled and very thin,' Diana told me. 'So when Yehudi walked into the room, it was truly shocking. He was so pink, so radiant and so sweet. He was a bit on the plump side, in fact, but he had such wonderful skin. That is what I remember most. We were not used to anyone with *colour* in their face, not after five years of greyness and war. And he had thick, golden hair and, truly, a kind of radiance. Like a glow-worm. Or do I mean a firefly? Somewhere between the two. I found out later that he glows all the time, night and day. A constant light, and I promise you I'm not exaggerating.'

Meanwhile, back in the Russian Tea Room:

DM: We had saved up a whole week's rations for the great occasion. After all, we already knew through our friends Dennison and Ingerson that Yehudi had been given a letter of introduction to us some fifteen years earlier. In fact, each time Yehudi had come to London, they had told him: "Do go and meet the Gould family," and he hadn't. So here he was, eating up a whole week's rations!'

YM: 'But I was discreet, wasn't I? I didn't overeat, did I?'

DM: 'No, no, I don't think you did, but you did look revoltingly prosperous. And we were all grey, like Bombay ducks. Thin, dry . . .'

YM: 'Now, now, don't exaggerate that, because . . .'

DM: 'But it's true!'

YM: 'Diana was sitting on a pouf, at the end of the room, beneath an elegant fireplace. I had never seen anything more beautiful. And I realized this was it. I realized it was only a matter of time . . .'

DM: 'Yes, pink cheeks and, shall I say, a little overweight.'

YM: 'Well, certainly not looking like an artist.'

DM: 'What? Oh come now. What does an *artist* look like?'

YM: 'Well, I was thinking that maybe I looked more like a successful stockbroker.'

DM: 'You mean that an artist should have a dirty beret and sandals!'

YM: 'Well, I do remember the food being delicious. Your mother must have been a marvellous cook.'

DM: 'Yes, and luckily that was before you got on one of your

eternal diets. *Nobody* had been more self-disciplined than I.
I never smoked, I never drank a thing. After all, I had been
trained as a dancer, so one had to watch one's figure like mad.
And then to be landed with Yehudi who would say, "You
mustn't touch white sugar"; "You mustn't touch white flour"!
And during the war! Jam, he told me, was a great sin. Butter
also. And when we got to know each other better *after* the
war, it was Quark! Sort of sour milk. Ugh! I shudder when I
think how much awful yoghurt I've eaten just to please him.
If you convince Yehudi that manure is good for you, it will
suddenly taste like ambrosia to him. I can't begin to tell you
the horrors I've swallowed in the last forty years in the name
of health!'

YM: 'Well, health, like yoga, irrigates the brain. Yoga also relieves
the heart of having to pump against gravity; it relieves pressure
on the legs.'

DM: '*And* makes him into the most obstinate man I have ever met.
I used to keep a little notebook at one point called "Grounds
for Divorce". But pretty soon the little notebook grew into a
telephone directory. But I think I've only thrown two breakfast
trays and one typewriter at you during the last forty years,
haven't I? So that's not *too* bad. I am, after all, half Irish.'

The Irish half originally came from Cork, where Diana's father's
family had made their 'fortune in booze' before settling in Paris.
Her father, Gerard, had been a diplomat, before dying of typhoid
after only five years of marriage. Her mother had been born Evelyn
Suart, in India, the daughter of a cavalry officer, but had been
despatched quite early to her mother who lived in Brussels and was
known as Goggo. Goggo, a Christian Scientist, decided that Miss
Evelyn was musical; by chance she knew Ysaÿe, and so arranged
for Miss Evelyn to have lessons with one of his assistants.
After Gerard's death, Evelyn had married again, to a Naval
Commander-in-Chief, Cecil Harcourt, and the young Diana had

been shipped from private school to private school, showing no academic inclinations whatsoever. In despair, her mother had eventually sent her – accompanied only by a Scottish nanny – to an establishment called Phoenix House, where she received ballet lessons from a retired ballerina with Diaghilev's company, Serafina Astafieva. Diana was then eight years old.

Fellow pupils happened to be Alicia Markova and Frederick Ashton, and soon the 'illiterate nitwit of a daughter' (Diana's own description of herself) was being taught by the famous Marie Rambert in Notting Hill Gate on the recommendation of Enrico Cecchetti, Diaghilev's ballet master. There, she partnered Ashton in his first ballet, 'Leda and the Swan', and was finally swept up by Diaghilev himself into the last season of his great Ballets Russes.

The 'stringbean' – '*la seule jeune fille que j'aimerais épouser*,' Diaghilev had said – soon learned the rigours of life on the road, such as the small hotels throughout Europe which somehow had not yet heard that Diaghilev rarely paid any bills. When Diaghilev died, Diana danced for Charles Cochran, the London West End impresario, auditioned for George Balanchine and performed 'L'Aprèsmidi d'un Faune' with Serge Lifar. Her apotheosis arrived when she came face to face with Bronislava Nijinska, the sister of Nijinsky. Feeling the force (and value) of such a link with the legendary past, Diana danced her heart out until 'blood came oozing through' one of her ballet shoes. Mercifully, the Second World War put a stop to the touring. Well, not quite, because somehow Diana managed to get to Cairo (the Opera House) in 1944, and subsequently to Bari following the liberation of southern Italy. Her energy seemed boundless, albeit at this time lacking purpose.

All that changed when she met Yehudi. 'I knew he was my destiny,' she says simply. 'It sounds arrogant, but it really isn't. In 1944 I did have several other misguided men who felt they'd like to marry me. But, after all, I had become a dancer because I understood very early that I couldn't live without music, and that had been my real true love. So when Yehudi returned to London in the summer of 1945 to work on the soundtrack of a film biography of the violinist Paganini being made by Landseer Films in Lime Grove Studios (later the BBC Current Affairs department), and called *The Magic Bow*, we began to see each other more regularly.'

Yehudi, Diana says, began to rely on her more and more for advice. 'I realized,' she told me, 'that he'd *never* had anyone to talk to,' a curious observation when one remembers the loving home movies of Yehudi and Nola's honeymoon. It is possible that the request for advice was at first nothing more than a discreet visiting card from the naturally reticent Yehudi to the naturally gregarious and louder-than-life Diana. Nonetheless, if it was advice he wanted, advice he got. He had now been asked to play Paganini himself, replacing none other than Stewart Granger, opposite Phyllis Calvert. Thankfully (according to Diana), the world was spared Yehudi's acting debut; the producers (and Diana) decided that Menuhin in a long wig and velvet kneepants was not exactly what the public was waiting for. Yehudi insisted that Diana help him with the script, however, just in case the producers saw the light. Diana had to repeat endlessly, 'I love you, I love you,' to enable Yehudi 'to feel his way into the part'. Yehudi/Paganini even had the line, 'I would like you to marry me', to which Diana/Phyllis Calvert had to reply: 'Oh, Nikkerlo, what gorgeous sounds you draw from that magic bow!'

Diana's innate musicality – and despite all the blather and Irish blarney with which she tends to flatten anything and anyone that crosses her path, there is no escaping her musical intelligence and instinct – soon brought her face to face with a being far removed from the overweight, pink-skinned archangel who just happened to have come to lunch. During the first months of their relationship, Diana was appearing at the Piccadilly Theatre in London, playing Michael Redgrave's mistress in *Jacobowsky and the Colonel*. Diana and Yehudi met every night after the show; and whenever possible Diana went to Yehudi's concerts which, during the war, were often in the afternoon. 'And then I remembered what had astonished me so much about his playing when I had first heard him in the Royal Albert Hall,' she told me, 'long before I met him. The average violinist scythes. But Yehudi never scythed, which is what I believe made audiences all over the world love him.'

'He always gave the feeling that he and his violin were one,' she went on, 'that the violin was simply a continuation of Yehudi, that what he wanted to say flowed straight down his arm and into his instrument. In 1945, however, I saw that there was something profoundly wrong. Underneath that sweet exterior, he seemed totally unsafe. Something had come between him and his violin; he didn't feel at home with it; he felt as if he was fighting it, as if the violin had become his enemy. His playing was absolutely detached, as if he didn't quite know what he was doing. He seemed to have fallen from a great height and smashed into pieces. Worse, he had begun to blame himself, begun to convince himself that he wasn't any longer capable of playing the violin as he had done before. Goodness knows what he must have been through. It must have been hell.'

Most of the Menuhin family agree that the years between Yehudi's first meeting with Diana in 1944 and their eventual marriage on 19 October 1947, were dark indeed. 'Everyone has their own version of what happened,' Diana's eldest son by Yehudi told me. 'But in truth there hasn't been much objective thought, although maybe "thought" is the wrong word.'

Nola was at last persuaded to allow her two children (Zamira and Krov) to spend the summer of 1947 with Diana. Poor Nola. So befuddled had her mind become that it seems she no longer had the stamina to fight for what was hers by right. From Yehudi's point of view, however, Diana rescued the children from a life of unhappiness, even squalor, and provided a security and perspective which otherwise might have been denied them. Before long, Zamira moved in completely (Yehudi says she 'ran away', having 'fallen in love with Diana'), while Krov returned to look after what he admits was his increasingly wayward mother.

Diana also attempted to repair the relationship between Yehudi and his parents, which had become estranged as the marriage to Nola had disintegrated. 'In this way, I can see now that I was confirmed as an adult,' Yehudi told me. 'Diana [was] not only fit for any responsibility,' Yehudi wrote later, 'she [was] incapable of not responding to a need.' Part of this responsibility, Krov told me, was that Diana 'felt it was her *duty* to isolate Yehudi from any part of the family which she believed threatened his well-being'. Undoubtedly Nola's drinking was one such threat, although soon it was anything to do with Nola. 'The best thing was to keep Yehudi away from the day-to-day problems of Nola's children,' Krov added. 'Maybe she felt that my presence, and my link with Nola, might be disturbing to Yehudi, might affect his playing, might prevent Humpty-Dumpty from having any chance of being put back together.' Yehudi claims that this notion of Krov's is 'blatantly untrue' and 'vindictive'.

Unfortunately, no one seems to have thought of asking Nola what she wanted: Nola, the wife, who, if she hadn't exactly been chosen for Yehudi by Marutha, was at least *the* wife. The fact that she had (according to Diana) begun to make her children's life wretched, failing even to clean and feed them properly, must have given Yehudi many troubled moments. But if he was now 'confirmed' as an adult, surely his gratitude should have been directed, at least in part, towards Nola? After all, as far as Yehudi was concerned, he had more or less run away from his parents to be with Nola; she had been the means of escape, even if he had eventually botched it. She had been in the beginning 'a bright white light which fell across my path', Yehudi told me. Alas, she had 'wished to continue her life of gaiety and conquests, reacting to every moment as it occurred, with not a thought for ... that imperative foresight so necessary to [my] highly sensitive and demanding career'. And for Nola?

'I did all my pregnancies touring,' Diana told me cheerfully, referring to her own children. 'I merely dropped the child wherever the violin was on the ninth month. The first (Gerard) was born in Edinburgh, during the Festival; the second (Jeremy) in San Francisco; and a third, also in San Francisco, but that one unfortunately did not survive the nine months' travel.' Their first home was the rebuilt and expanded Alma, where Yehudi had lived 'unhappily' with Nola but where Yehudi and Diana were now to stay for eight years. In other words, not far from Moshe and Marutha. Indeed, with the birth of the first child, Diana became convinced that, as with Krov and Zamira, 'the wretched child' would have to be given an unpronounceable Russian name to please Marutha. Secretly, she had decided to call the child Smith, regardless of its sex. At least that was safe. In the event, the first-born was called after Diana's father, although his nickname was always to be Mita (a Russianization of Smith). It was an agonizing birth, for mother and child, and 'the poor child … hauled out … battered and blue' became known as Smithy.

Smithy soon discovered what it was to be the son of a nomad. After Edinburgh, mother and son moved back to London, thence a month later to Paris; via Honolulu (without child) to Alma in California. Then to Rome, back via New York to Central and South America, Yehudi 'cheerfully catapulting us from town to town'; South Africa, via Alan Paton (*Cry, the Beloved Country* had just been published) and General Smuts; back to London via Israel; 'If the traitor Menuhin comes to Israel, we will kill him as we killed Bernadotte last year,' had read one welcoming message. And all this before Smithy was three.

Jeremy, the second son and today an accomplished pianist, was born in Stanford Hospital on 2 November 1951, while the foghorns were blowing repeatedly across the Bay Area. He was christened in Rochester Cathedral in England (where else?), because 'the bishop wanted to be one of the godfathers,' Diana told me. Jeremy, 'a solid, beaming infant' (Diana's description), grabbed the bishop's spectacles during the ceremony, thus causing the priest to lose his place completely in the prayer book; he then squeezed the bishop's nose and giggled a lot. Also present was the thirteen-year-old Zamira. 'Up to the age of twelve,' Yehudi told me, 'her early life was really hideous.' To all who would listen, Zamira announced, characteristically but ominously, that 'she wanted to be a child, before it was too late.'

Each child seemed to bring a new resolution in Yehudi to become the ideal father, and with the birth of Jeremy he decided that in future Diana should stay put with the children and not try and follow him on the road. 'Diana was determined to correct Nola's complaint that I was a poor father,' Yehudi told me. But the subsequent separation of the family unit inevitably brought its problems. Maybe these were the necessary outcome of a peripatetic existence, and if so Yehudi made every effort to devote himself to his children's upbringing as and when he could. Family picnics became an essential part of his schedule. Today, however, Yehudi often recalls the problem in terms of his *own* isolation. '*Whether or not* [my italics] the children lost anything [by his frequent absences],' he remembered, 'it was a loss to me.' And the loss to the *children*?

What sustained the marriage, then as now, was the rapier-like repartee that fired the indignation of both partners. Even an hour spent in their company can be an exhausting experience, especially when they are attempting to recall their early years together. 'One of the difficulties,' Yehudi told me conspiratorially, 'is that when I feel something very deeply, I often find it quite hard to express it in words. And I'm sorry to say that I think my children hold this against me.' (Turning to Diana): 'I don't know whether they hold it against you too, darling?'

DM: *What* do they hold against you? They adore you.'

YM: 'I know. But the fact that . . .'

DM: 'Don't talk nonsense.'

YM: 'No, no. The fact that I don't react with effusion and exuber-ance. In my own childhood, for instance, I remember a terrible disappointment when I was six or seven. I had said something unforgivable, and my parents so shamed me that I determined at that very moment that I would never, never say anything until I had thought it through.'

DM: 'Well, you've certainly made up for it since.' (To me:) 'He's so balanced, he's like a gyrocompass. But I think one can live with that. At least he doesn't come swinging in on the chandelier every day.'

YM: 'Well, you see, that's because our lives are like spinning tops. Nothing is permanent. Nothing can stay in one place. I suppose it's not much different from the life of an airplane pilot, or a naval officer who is constantly on patrol in a submarine . . .'

DM (interrupting him): 'You don't have a girl in every port, like the sailors, do you?'

YM: 'Well, not *every* port, but I have acquired a remarkable collection of ladies in different parts of the world.'

DM: 'Who?'

YM: 'Well, there's Agnes Albert . . .'

DM: 'But she's over *eighty*!'

YM: 'And then there's Berlin. Lady Cholmondeley . . .'

DM: 'Ah, she's merely a cover-up for all the others who are three decades younger. Minimum.'

YM: 'Oh, no. Only *two* decades, darling. Well, maybe fifteen years. Women have a lot to teach men, really.'

DM: 'Well, I can't think why women find you so fascinating *now*. You look like one of those photographs of old ladies with their teeth taken out. Their chins reach their noses, and their noses reach their foreheads. You're beginning to look like that.'

YM: 'Oh, well, there's always my nice brown eyes.'

DM: 'Exactly!' (To me:) 'One of the many, very nice things about Yehudi is – as I once said to him after we'd been married a few years – that he never thinks of himself or his clothes. I once asked him, for instance, what were the colour of his eyes? And he said brown! And I said, "Well, they've been blue for thirty-two years."' (To Yehudi, and shouting:) 'Never think of yourself, do you?'

YM: 'Well, I am rather pleased with my new silk ties ...'

DM: 'Oh yes, very chic. But when I *first* met you, your clothes were deplorable. In fact, poor lamb, you hardly had any.'

YM: 'Well, I always had you as a constant example ...'

DM: 'Even now, he doesn't dress properly. But he is very slightly colour-blind. You can't tell the difference between red and green, can you?'

YM: 'Oh yes, I can.'

DM: 'Well then, you've got even less excuse for putting on all those very odd ties and suits. I've always excused you on the grounds that you were colour-blind!'

YM: 'But I thought you approved of the last tie I put on with this suit.'

DM: 'Pure chance.' (To me:) 'Never ask Yehudi facts. Not even the time of day, nor even what he's playing tonight. I once took him down to a concert hall not long after we were married, and he unpacked in his dressing room and began practising. Soon the manager of the hall came in and said to Yehudi, "Why are you practising *that*?" "But it's the Mozart G Major Concerto," replied Yehudi, "and I'm playing it tonight." "Oh no you're not," said the manager. "You're playing the Mozart *A* Major!" "Oh," said Yehudi, and promptly changed key. That was just twenty minutes before he was due to go on stage! Didn't you, darling? Never mind. Life is full of surprises.'

YM: 'Well, despite the schedule and the fact that everything is planned months, even years ahead, I love to keep an element of spontaneity.'

DM: 'So *that's* what it's called!'

YM: 'Yes, that is what it's called.'

DM: 'You mean that every time you're late, and every time you tell me something that isn't correct, I must learn never to listen to your first answer! Because that's just a throwaway; your spontaneity.'

YM: 'That's right.'

DM: 'After forty-something years! Now I know.'

YM: 'Yes, that's right.'

DM: 'Thank you, darling. Stupid of me. Oh well, hope springs eternal.'

YM: 'Well, life *is* curious. I feel like an airplane, well on its way, perhaps nearing the end of its journey and nearing its destination. Therefore it's very light; it has very little fuel left ...'

DM: 'Oh come!'

YM: 'Yes, it's true. It goes faster and faster, higher and higher, and ...'

DM: 'You sound like a glider going up to heaven! Where's all this Old Testament rubbish coming from?'

YM: 'But you see, we don't really have a destination. We can't really say that we're going to land in such-and-such a place.'

DM: 'Yehudi Menuhin! I never knew you *thought* like this. After all this time together! Is this something which occurred to you during your last tour? I always thought you were so gloriously vague, just occasionally coming down from Cloud Nine, focussing a bit, then setting off once again on your travels.'

YM: 'But I *am* gloriously vague.'

DM: 'Well, why are you suddenly talking about airplanes with no fuel? Who do you think you are suddenly? The angel Gabriel?'

YM: 'Well, I ...'

DM: 'You sound like an out-of-commission Concorde!'

And so on. These conversations can continue for hours, appear to be totally spontaneous, are relentlessly subversive, often barbed, clearly very loving, and most importantly the life-blood of a hectic partnership that must have come like a bucket of cold water dumped all over the 'radiating pink' Yehudi when they had first met. Members of the family told me that these exchanges merely illustrate their nickname for Yehudi and Diana – 'Sir Hypocrite and Lady Monologue'. Whatever else, the relationship with Diana was and is a far cry from the pampered world of Marutha and Moshe, although, according to Krov, it was never quite the childlike, obsessive love affair that Yehudi had experienced with Nola. Yehudi would deny this, of course. 'The blatant and recurring evidence of Nola's infidelity,' he told me, 'her inability to cope with the essential needs of an artist; all this meant there had not been the slightest chance of a permanent bond. In fact, no bond between us had ever been properly forged. Diana, on the other hand, was (and is) everything I needed.'

'When I first met Yehudi,' Diana told me with relish, 'he *never* thought, and not just because his parents had always looked after him. To this day, he prefers lying on his palanquin and having everything done for him. Just floating along, bless him. He *is* calculating, but he hates persuading, unless he's trying to persuade someone else about the latest dotty idea that's come into his head. But not about anything to do with himself. If you try to persuade him about that, his eyes just glaze over. Unfortunately one really can't live one's entire life in this way,' Diana added, 'at least not if you have a family. And this attitude cannot, and could not, compensate for something that had gone seriously wrong in his life, which I realized even if I didn't quite know what it was. I *smelt* it.'

She must have heard it also, because his playing began to acquire those characteristics which have occasionally bedevilled his performances ever since. In fairness, some remarkable recordings exist from the decade following the Second World War, most notably the Beethoven Violin Concerto, conducted by Furtwängler, never surpassed in interpretation and performance, and rarely equalled since, by *any* violinist. But this is perhaps an exception. Getting all the notes right, and in the correct order, had not been Yehudi's strongest card for several years, but according to Diana even his legendary intuition now seemed to be deserting him. 'Whatever it was that troubled him,' Diana told me, 'had got so deeply into him that he didn't want to examine it. He never does examine; he doesn't like taking things apart. So he didn't want to know why the violin was no longer his friend.'

Diana convinced herself that the best cure was to force him to do all those little things which most of us take for granted. If he was going to *tour* South America, for instance, he might as well take some time off and *see* South America. 'An ultimatum was an ultimatum,' Yehudi remembered. Suddenly Peru meant more than the next hotel, the next concert hall. Peru meant Cuzco and Machu Picchu. And much though Diana has complained subsequently about the rigours of that particular journey, especially into the interior of Peru, at the time she insisted that they travel the hard way. From Cuzco along a bumpy, dusty road, in a car with no tyres, for over four hours. Thence up a tangled ravine, dragging their luggage with them. Thence sleeping on wooden-plank beds with sandbag mattresses. Not quite the luxury to which Yehudi had become accustomed.

A similar dose of shock medicine was administered when Yehudi went back to South Africa in 1950. His earlier visit in 1935 had passed without incident, almost as if Yehudi had been unaware of any internal political problems. Admittedly, apartheid as a state system had not yet been invented, although racial privilege and black resentment were already much in evidence. By 1950, however, these prejudices had been translated by the national government into legal repression, in response to which a schoolteacher, Alan Paton, had published his tale of two families, *Cry, the Beloved Country*. As we have seen, Yehudi's experiences in Belsen and post-war Germany had aroused his social conscience, but it was Diana who goaded the previously apolitical Yehudi into an unusual confrontation.

Yehudi had telephoned Alan Paton to express admiration for the novel and ask if there was anything he could do to help. Come and play for the blacks in my school at Diepkloof, was the reply. Yehudi obliged, accompanied on a broken upright by his colleague Marcel

Gazelle. In return, the black children offered Yehudi a selection of Christmas hymns. By all accounts it was a touching and innocent occasion, except that innocence was not a quality which the South African police could tolerate. Yehudi's South African management told him that this impromptu concert was outside the terms of their agreement, and therefore not allowed. Yehudi protested that, since young black Africans were forbidden to attend his concerts, his little recital was of no commercial value to the agent.

The agent continued to grumble, whereupon Yehudi informed him that in future he would give duplicate concerts, one for blacks and one for whites. Thus, at a social centre in Sophiatown, one of the black shantytowns near Johannesburg, Yehudi became the first white international soloist that black South Africa had ever heard. The agent was not amused. Yehudi was summoned to the agent's office, and told that he was to be sued for breach of contract. Pending settlement, all his fees in South Africa were to be forfeited. Yehudi lost his temper and stormed out, putting at risk his entire concert future in South Africa, since his agent was the most powerful in the land. The agent subsequently apologized but, as Yehudi remembered later, 'Regrettably, my ... victory left no lasting mark on South African history.' This was not the Yehudi of the pre-war years.

'The quicksands of doubt' (Yehudi's description) had to be overcome. There came the realization that, as far as his violin technique was concerned, intellect would have to replace intuition. 'One day my fingers had their old reassurance,' he remembered, 'another they fumbled.' The 'search for enlightenment', as he called it, became systematic. For the first time in his life he studied Dounis' classic books, *Technique of the Violin* and *The Independence of the Fingers*. He read Carl Flesch's *The Art of Violin-Playing*. He had the honesty to discuss his problems with fellow violinists such as Joseph Szigeti.

Meanwhile, he studied the laws of physics and became fascinated by yoga, all in pursuit of a lost innocence which, he believed, had endowed his gift. Taking lessons from a young guru called Iyengar,

Yehudi learned to breathe deeply and quietly, to celebrate the body rather than debase it, to untie the knots which had begun to strangle him, and thus find his way back to a childhood whose security he felt he had lost.

We shall return to Yehudi's yoga later, but the panacea he felt it offered was probably valuable only in so far as he believed that that is what it was, whereas the security which his relationship with Diana had begun to give him was of paramount importance. I am sure he has never underestimated this element of life with Diana, or if he has ever been tempted to underestimate it, Diana would have very quickly thrust its significance back under his nose. It is clear to me that the heady mixture of tough, abrasive, no-nonsense bullying which she administered, together with all the loving attention to those aspects of his life which seem not to interest him – she still combs his hair in the dressing room before every concert – worked the cure more effectively than any amount of yoga.

Although musical, she could not help him repair his violin technique, but she could (and did) help rebuild his inner confidence, and from that, she hoped, would come a restoration of his violin-playing. Yehudi now maintains that, wounding though his divorce from Nola and his visit to Belsen were, the real problem with his violin technique was that (as Ysaÿe had indicated) he had never practised his scales and arpeggios when young. But no musician – singer, dancer, composer or instrumentalist – is unaffected by their state of health or mind, a fact which I am certain Diana understood very well.

It is easy to criticize the extent to which her crusading zeal damaged other relationships, and to hold her responsible for the painful isolation which some of his children began to feel. In truth, she attempted to be a devoted and loving mother to *all* Yehudi's children, including and especially Krov 'in spite of having had his mind poisoned by Nola' (Yehudi). Diana never forgot a Christmas or a birthday, Yehudi told me, and 'welcomed Krov, his wife and little son every summer in our house. It was Diana who told Krov to find the farm which is now their home, and told me to buy it for him. But, later, did he [Krov] ever write to us?' Yehudi asked me. 'Or ever reply to Diana's letters, or thank her for her regular presents? We don't even know what his handwriting looks like.'

Whatever else, it seems that Diana protected Yehudi not just from his apparently ungrateful family, but also from certain newspaper reviewers whose unpleasant remarks made them marked men for decades. It is easy to overlook the extent to which the Yehudi Menuhin who is known throughout the world today, or at least the *image* of Yehudi Menuhin, is principally her creation.

Their visit to India in 1952 was, in many ways, the culmination of her early work, and a turning point. Yehudi and Diana arrived in New Delhi at the invitation of Prime Minister Nehru, 'feeling like two old bags of biscuit crumbs' (Diana's description). Nehru was obviously anxious to promote his new country in every way possible, but while he wanted the very best – musicians, singers, theatre, cinema – he knew he could not afford it. Characteristically, Yehudi not only volunteered to spend two months in India, but offered to give the entire proceeds from his concerts (less expenses) to the famine fund in Madras, where over a million people had died the previous year.

Yehudi and Diana were met at the airport by Nehru's daughter, Indira, and taken to Flagstaff House, once the headquarters of the British Army in India, now the Prime Minister's official residence. Diana noticed the Axminster carpets ('very bank manager's Streatham'), whereas Yehudi immediately sensed that in Nehru he had encountered a truly kindred spirit, a man who never hesitated to speak the truth, no matter whom it hurt; 'one of the few honest men of state our times have known,' Yehudi told me. Before dinner (English food, to Yehudi's immense disappointment), the conversation turned to yoga, and Nehru challenged Yehudi ('in his best Harrovian manner') to stand on his head – the sirshasana. Yehudi replied that he was only a beginner but, so as not to offend his host, volunteered to do as he was asked. Whereupon Nehru, remonstrating with Yehudi that he must do better, also stood on his head. At this point, with the Prime Minister of India and a world-famous violinist both upended, the major-domo arrived to announce: 'Dinner is served.'

Yehudi thought Diana was being less than gracious when she told Nehru that she found him to be not the great Brahmin of repute, but sometimes little more than 'an irascible English lawyer'. 'That's probably why the British put me in prison so often,' Nehru replied. 'If we hadn't had the sense to do that,' said Diana, 'you would never have had the time to write all those books!' It was vintage Diana, and exactly the right antidote to all that Indian mumbo-jumbo which passes as Eastern philosophy, and which inevitably had begun to intrigue Yehudi.

The smells and sounds of India are, of course, utterly and instantly irresistible, even to the most grizzled traveller. What takes time is the adjustment to a different pace of living in India. At the outset one misinterprets this casualness as sloth or indifference, and no doubt the bustling Diana would have had little patience with the apparently slow-moving way of life Indians find attractive. But, after the opening concert (a recital with Marcel Gazelle as accompanist, and introduced by Amrit Kaur, a legendary freedom-fighter against the British), Diana realized that here was an atmosphere in which she hoped Yehudi could be healed; if not restored to the wholeness of his childhood, at least sufficiently healed that the future could be faced with a little more optimism.

In the first place, Yehudi experienced what amounted to a reincarnation. In spite of his Jewishness, and the traditions that being a Jew entailed, Yehudi had always felt (he says) homeless. Partly this must have come about because of his wandering childhood, and the lack of any place he felt he could truly call home; born an American, later an honorary Swiss citizen, now a naturalized Englishman while retaining American and Swiss passports, it is easy to see how he became rootless. Partly, as we have seen, this feeling of homelessness had been exacerbated by the loss of Nola and the agony of Belsen, which had wrecked whatever security his childhood had given him. 'All my life I had longed to feel underfoot the solid ground of the past,' he now says, and India, with its timeless majesty ('a ladder with religion on every rung'), showed him a world whose values were beyond anything he had been taught, either by Marutha or by his own experience. 'To belong to such a continuity relieves the individual,' he wrote later, an idea which in a sense has become the motto for the rest of his life. Retrospectively, we can see that, in so far as it is possible to understand a miracle, this idea is a key to his great musical gift.

The means by which one reaches a state of being wherein belonging to such a continuity becomes inevitable are, of course, complex and tortuous. What is clear is that a secure violin technique is not part of the process. Another and more intriguing clue is offered by Indian music itself, described by Yehudi as 'having no predetermined beginning or end, but flowing without interruption through the fingers of the composer-performer'. In the most important section of his autobiography, Yehudi writes of this experience as being 'in the presence of creation'.

Even in 1952, Ravi Shankar was the prince among sitar players. His introduction of India's music to Yehudi was a profound musical revelation. Today, with our instant access to all cultures of the world through CDs and television films, it is hard to imagine a time when, for most Western audiences – even those well-disposed towards anything contemporary – culture meant something European, preferably dead and, as far as music was concerned, beginning with B, as in Bach, Beethoven or Brahms. This was, after all, the main reason Yehudi had first come to Europe from San Francisco; without a success in Berlin, or London, or Paris, playing Bach, Beethoven or Brahms, an international violinist in the 1930s had just not arrived.

But Indian music, with its quarter-tones and endlessly variable rhythms, has a richness and variety beyond the understanding of the Bs. It is not better than, and certainly not greater than (as some devotees would want us to believe) European classical music. Nor is the fact that 'its purpose is to redefine the soul and discipline the body' philosophically much different from the 'purpose' (in so far as it has a purpose) of a Beethoven symphony. More important is the emphasis that Indian music places on individual creation. Yehudi sees a parallel in this to society itself. 'Whereas the development of Western society has been towards the community,' he says, 'with individuals freely accepting certain restraints on their freedom for what is hoped to be the collective good of the whole, Indian society – and religion and culture – has always cherished the individual and his harmony with other individuals. Nehru always told me that this was why India, as a state, was ungovernable, although one should always try. "It could not be abandoned," he told me, "but no one could cope with it."' In other words, 'to reach our apogee,' Yehudi wrote, 'we have to subjugate our natures, then to free them'. It seems to me that the journey from child prodigy to broken man, and thence to the Yehudi Menuhin of today, bears witness to the truth of this dictum and also to the extent to which Yehudi has struggled throughout his life to achieve peace of mind.

Diana, whether she grasped the philosophical complexity of this journey or not, was the essential helpmate. Too easily Yehudi might have slithered into a kind of spiritual nirvana of joss sticks and yoga and never again been taken seriously. As it is, he puts pen to paper on the smallest pretext, scribbling reams on 'A Vision of Europe', or 'Heaven on Earth', or 'Art and Science as Related Concepts'. What he writes is never less than interesting; frequently, his essays elaborate challenging ideas which, even if they are culled from other sources, at least have the imprimatur of a world figure.

But words such as 'wonderful' and 'beauty' and 'truth' abound in his writings, with the result that any philosophical merit in what he has to say is squandered by a constant feeling of gosh-golly. Diana's cold-water good sense, on the other hand, has prevented Yehudi from disappearing completely down a Hindu plug-hole. The transcendental aspects of India were not for her; what concerned her more were the rats which constantly tugged at her mosquito net at night. 'Aching and sticky and mutinous' after a particularly arduous journey to see 'a very important Jain statue', she discovered that the said statue was painted in 'hideous colours ... [with] ruby-red lips and the simper of a maudlin drunk'. One can be sure that she told Yehudi exactly what she was thinking.

And when Yehudi began to indulge his passion for Indian health foods, Diana's Irish temper exploded. 'Leather toast and manure coffee' were bad enough. But one day, during a car journey, 'Yehudi saw a fruit he had not heard of,' she said, hanging from a tree like 'an indecent football ... with a hairy umbilical cord'. Their host told him that although the fruit was edible, it was not to be recommended because of its unpleasant smell. Nothing, of course, would deter Yehudi and of course the fruit, once opened, stank. The subsequent journey, said Diana, was like 'travelling in a per-ambulating armpit'.

Nor were Yehudi's concerts given unqualified approval by Diana. In Madras, Yehudi insisted on playing the Bartók Violin Sonata, hoping that its dissonance would appeal to the ears of those well-accustomed to quarter-tones. Instead, says Diana, she had to endure the Governor of Madras constantly wringing his hands and com-plaining about these 'terrible noises'. Nonetheless, the terrible noises raised $38,000 for the famine fund (half a million dollars today), an enormous individual contribution from which no amount of 'shabby flowered carpets' in their guest house, chairs with 'Baptist chapel backs' and 'bloated purple armchair[s] looking like fat alcoholics in the last stages of DTs' could ultimately detract.

During the next twenty years, Yehudi returned to India whenever he could, and in 1966 brought Ravi Shankar to the Bath Festival, of which Yehudi was at that time the musical director. It was thus Yehudi, rather than Beatle George Harrison, who brought Shankar to the attention of the general public, and whenever Shankar and Yehudi appeared on stage together to play raga duets, the fashion-conscious sixties saw this musical fusion as further convincing evidence of a new age. It was of course no such thing, except that George Harrison thought so, not least because Yehudi's technique did not seem to match Shankar's virtuosity. Once again, however, Yehudi's instinctive understanding of musical structure and meaning saw him through, and some inventive and pleasing recordings were made. If not exactly great music, the fact that it happened at all proved an important influence on a generation of young violinists, such as the English virtuoso Nigel Kennedy. Later associations with such as the French jazz violinist, Stéphane Grappelli, were equally important in the development of Yehudi as a man (rather than just as a musician), but none could match Shankar and what he represented philosophically.

Yehudi's life changed radically after India. He was tired of travel and needed time, as he said, to 'put down roots'. No doubt Diana's dislike of unnecessary discomfort was an important factor. The death, at birth, of a third child seemed an omen. Several near disasters in airplanes caused both of them to renounce air travel for almost nine years, so changing the pattern of Yehudi's touring. The death in 1953 of three musical colleagues in plane crashes – Ginette Neveu, Jacques Thibaud and William Kapell – seemed the limit. But when Yehudi announced that air travel was not for him, quite simply because it wasn't safe enough, there was (in England, at least) a public outcry which, in its turn, provoked furious letters of support of his stand. 'Dammit, Menuhin,' one letter read, 'travel by camel if you want to.'

The permanent move from California to London was still to come, as was the chalet in Gstaad which, if anywhere could be called home, was to offer Yehudi the most sanctuary. But the important change was that Yehudi began to combine his missionary zeal with his mainstream musical activities. He also stopped worrying about his technique, accepting that it would never be quite what it had been and that, ultimately, this probably didn't matter. Russia, for instance, and the Russian Empire now started to preoccupy him. It was, after all, in some senses his homeland. A return visit to

Leipzig in what was then East Germany, where he was thrown off a train by the border police because he lacked the appropriate visa, proved emotional and exhausting. Playing in the rebuilt Gewandhaus – an 'ugly experience' – when some of the players still remembered Yehudi's visit in 1929; insisting that the doors be opened at the end of the concert to let in the crowds of young people who had been unable to get the 'official tickets'; despatching an orchestra official on a bicycle to collect more orchestral parts so that Yehudi and the orchestra could perform yet more encores – all this seems reminiscent of the glory days of his youth.

The journey to Poland in 1957 – Yehudi and Diana's first of many – was also symptomatic of Yehudi's new hard-won freedom. No matter the half-destroyed buildings, many still derelict after twelve years of Communist rule; no matter that the Grande Suite of their hotel in Warsaw had a lavatory/bathroom which, as far as Diana could see, had previously been occupied by half a dozen incontinent horses – 'I opened the door to the bathroom and staggered back, retching' (Diana); no matter the rehearsals in near freezing temperatures, causing Yehudi to blow constantly on his fingers when not playing; no matter the state agent who suddenly announced to Yehudi that, somehow, mysteriously, Yehudi's fee was 'not available', either in hard currency or in zlotys. The passion of the audience, the unbreakable spirit of all those Poles whom Yehudi and Diana encountered, and the optimism with which the Poles seemed to be facing an uncertain future, all spoke volumes. It was as if Yehudi had discovered his true role in life at last.

His place in musical history was assured. He had suffered, no more than most perhaps, in terms of personal unhappiness. He had blamed himself, although others had tried to absolve him of any real responsibility for what had happened to Nola. After all, Yehudi himself was 'tempted to call [what happened] crimes'.

It was Diana, and what Yehudi perceived as the mystical enlightenment of India, that had begun to stick Humpty-Dumpty back together again. If the violin was no longer an enemy, ways still had to be found to make his violin truly his friend again. With Diana's guidance, he was being transformed – and transforming himself – into a man with a mission, a man who was more than just a musician, a man who was in effect becoming an institution.

6

The Institution

'ONCE the Herbal Society rang me up,' Diana told me. '"The Herbal Society?" I said. Yes, the Herbal Society. "We want Mr Menuhin to come down to the Houses of Parliament and plead our cause. We wish to protest the use of certain chemicals in herbicides, and we feel that Mr Menuhin would be the appropriate spokesman." So I said: "But why Menuhin? He's a *violinist*." "Oh," they said, "because he's the most persuasive man on earth, and we know that he loves organic food and never eats anything with synthetics in it." "All right," I said reluctantly. So down he goes to the Houses of Parliament *and* he pleads their cause *and* he wins the day!

'Yehudi has become a handout boy,' Diana continued with that special mixture of truculence and approval that is sometimes hard to fathom. 'People ring him up for everything. The Home for Old Tired Bicycles. Who else but Yehudi? "Yes, darling," he asks me. "Who is it?" "The Home for Old Tired Bicycles," I reply. "There's something wrong with old tired bicycles, and they want you to speak on their behalf." And he does.

'He's the world's greatest seducer,' Diana went on, 'and without knowing it. Because he has no *line*, you see. No particular axe to grind. People can smell out professional lobbyists a mile away, or those who are seeking to gain profit from anything which they are supporting. But not Yehudi. Take this week alone, for instance. First week of February. It was supposed to be our month off. No, I learn only yesterday, tomorrow is Durham. "Durham?" I say.

1. Yehudi aged ten, on SS *Rochambeau*, before performing as solo violinist with the Lamoreux Symphony Orchestra in Paris

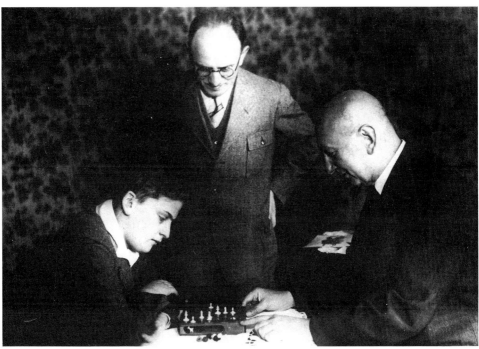

2. Yehudi with Fritz Busch, New York, 1926
3. Yehudi aged thirteen playing chess, Moshe Menuhin standing

4. Yehudi and Marutha in London, February 1938

5. Yehudi with Hephzibah and Yaltah, on their return to America, 8 March 1938

6. Nola and Yehudi on their wedding day, 26 May 1938
7. Yehudi and Nola, 3 March 1939

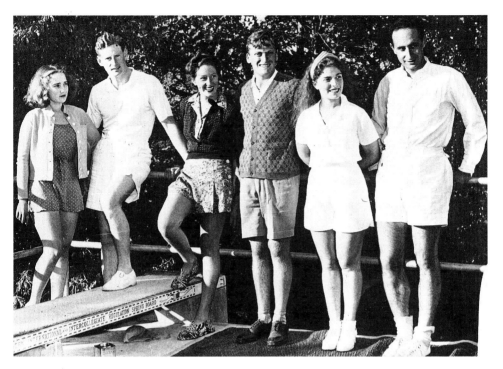

8. The three married Menuhins in California. *Left to right:* Hephzibah and Lindsay
Nicholas, Nola and Yehudi, Yaltah and William Stix
9. Nola, Yehudi and Zamira aged six weeks, 1939

10. Recital at the Albert Hall, 20 November 1938

11. Diana, 1940
12. Yehudi and Diana, 1958

13. Yehudi and Hephzibah, 1961

14. Zamira with Yehudi at her wedding to Fou Ts'ong, Hampstead Register Office, 1960

15. Yehudi and seven-year-old Gerard, 1956
16. Yehudi and Jeremy, 1964

17. Adrian Boult and Yehudi, 1944
18. Sir Thomas Beecham and Yehudi, 1955

19. Ravi Shankar, Diana and Yehudi, Delhi, 1952
20. Yehudi and David Oistrakh, 1963

21. Yehudi at seventy-five

"Yes, Durham," he says. "Oh well," I say, "I'll come with you because Durham is just about the only cathedral in England I have never seen." "We'll have to get up early," he says, "because the rehearsal with the orchestra is at lunchtime, and Durham is three hundred miles north of London. But we can always take the train."

'Then we learn that there has been an accident on the railway line *south* from Durham, so the line is blocked,' Diana says. 'Don't worry, we are told, the Bishop will send a car. "May I ask," I say, "*why* are we going to Durham when this is supposed to be your month off?" "Oh ... er ... don't know," he says behind hooded eyelids. Well, of course he knows perfectly well. He's playing to raise money for the cathedral, but he can't bring himself to say it, not even to me. This is the seven-*thousandth* cathedral that is standing because Yehudi has played for it!

'He's more than a man; he's an institution,' Diana continues relentlessly. 'He's president, or patron, or founder, or member, of over three hundred organizations. We keep a list; we *have* to, otherwise we would all become totally confused. It's over fifteen pages long, everything from Friends of the Earth to UNICEF. And it requires a whole team of people, including me, to try and keep pace with all that he is expected to do. But the incredible thing is that he is never late for anything important, although that does sometimes take a bit of managing. For ordinary appointments, on the other hand, he's *always* late because he can never be told that it *does* take a little time to get from one appointment to the next. Thus he makes appointments on the hour, every hour. "But darling," I say. "One is north of London, the other is *south* of London." Or, "One is in Paris, the other is in Brazil." "Oh yes," he says, grim-faced. "That's true."

'And yet he likes to think he's the most efficient person on earth (efficient as far as his own time is concerned!), so that he can spend every free moment worrying about backward children, or misplaced persons, or Africans, or Israel. Or just going to sleep. Yehudi really is the dormouse in the teapot,' Diana tells me. 'His *natural* being is when he's asleep. If he can't sleep twelve hours out of every twenty-four, he begins to totter. If I say, for instance, that you've got twenty minutes before CBS, SBC or TEP are coming, he will just lie on the floor and go to sleep – just like that. Eighteen out of the twenty minutes he will be sound asleep, and then wake up, utterly refreshed.

'Yehudi is the easiest man in the world to gain access to, because he never seems able to say no. Our secretary gives us a daily schedule,' Diana continues, 'which is often the only way I am able to find out what is happening. And so on this schedule I see: 10 am Mr Waverly Hacker. "May I know," I say with a tinge of sarcasm, "who is Mr Waverly Hacker?" Immediately the lids go down, the hooded lids of a lizard. "Come on," I say, "*who* is it?" "Er . . . er . . . don't know," comes the reply eventually. "Well, perhaps you could find out," I say. "Maybe you could ask yourself who it is." "Oh, all right," he says.

'"And *who*," I say, pressing the point, 'is Mrs Gfoops, at 11 am?" Rattle of eyes behind the lids. "Well, does *anybody* know?" I say. So I ring up the secretary and enquire who is Mr Waverly Hacker. "Oh," she says brightly, "that's a man who has a new proposal for peace between the Palestinians and the Israelis, and he wants to come and discuss it with Yehudi." "Oh yes," admits Yehudi. "Actually," he says with a little smile of apology, "it was *my* idea," and then beams like a little boy with a new toy.

'"All right," I say, "and *who* is Mrs Gfoops?" "Oooh," he says, still grinning. "*She's* a woman who's got a wonderful idea for a page-turner." "A *page*-turner?" say I.

'The front door bell rings, and a *very* strange lady comes in with an enormous contraption in a suitcase, which she is told to take upstairs to the studio. Another ring at the front door bell. "Who is it?" Yehudi asks cheerily. "Oh, this is the boy you're giving a lesson to. I hope you haven't forgotten," which of course he has. "Oh well," says Yehudi, "do tell him to come up." "He *can't* come up," I say with increasing exasperation, "because the page-turner and her machinery are in the studio." "Oh, we'll be finished in a minute," says Yehudi.

'So then we hear this terrible grinding, followed by an enormous crash. It turned out that the page-turning mechanism had to be clamped to the side of a music stand and operated by a pedal with your foot. But of course it was much too heavy for a normal music stand, so the moment you pressed the pedal, the whole thing became unbalanced and fell over. Crash. Obvious, I would have thought, to anyone except Yehudi and Mrs Gfoops.

'Down she comes a few minutes later, Mrs Gfoops, muttering apologies, but with a distinct look of failure on her face, and up goes the boy for his lesson. Ching Fung,' Diana says, 'or something like that, from Korea. Or China. They're *always* called Ching Fung and they *all* come from Korea or China. And so the morning goes on, and on. Finally I say to our cook/housekeeper that she'd better put the lunch back in the oven because who knows when we'll be eating. That's one reason why we *never* have soufflés in this house. They'd be in and out of the oven like demented yo-yos and end up looking like someone's old hat.

'Eventually, Yehudi appears for lunch, puts a sheet on the ground, lies down and is gone. Sound of heavy snoring,' says Diana, 'and all of us have to tiptoe round him until Mr Waverly Hacker appears who, of course, has a completely dotty idea which Yehudi listens to very patiently for about twenty minutes and who then storms out because he cannot make Yehudi agree with him. "It doesn't look as if you met on equal terms," I say to Yehudi later. "Oh," says Yehudi, "the trouble is he doesn't understand a thing about the problems, and he went away very dissatisfied. But he did get a few of my ideas I hope, so it was not a complete waste of time." "Well," I say, "now that's over, perhaps you could go upstairs and do a little practice?" "Ah yes," he says, as if it were the last thing in the world to occur to him, "what a nice idea!"'

'Yehudi does go romping off with the most extraordinary crooks from time to time, don't you darling?' Diana told me over lunch with Yehudi. 'Well,' he replied, 'I am aware that occasionally people *are* taking me for a ride. But I suppose I am not against the somewhat immoral principle of giving people enough rope to hang themselves.' 'But Menuhin,' Diana interrupts, 'that's perfectly horrible. Honestly! You're just saying that.' And then to me: 'He's just saying that, you know. He likes to appear sophisticated after the act. He *always* trusts people, because he always thinks that *everything* is redeemable and *everybody* is redeemable. And it's part of *my* job to stop him from being totally disillusioned over and over again.' 'Well, I'm just not suspicious,' Yehudi replies defensively. 'That much is true. I *want* to trust everyone, and I suppose that does sometimes lead to problems.'

Yehudi's 'institutional' life began as long ago as 1925 when the first newspaper reviews of his playing began to speak of him as a property rather than a person. He was a 'second Mozart' (why not a first Menuhin?); he had 'a duty' (aged nine!) to his American public. One critic spoke of violin virtuosi as 'uncanny little folk', although Menuhin 'differs from the majority of his kind in that he is not dark, but very fair. Blond prodigies are said to be as rare as white elephants or dead donkeys' (sic). A contemporary radio joke went as follows: a priest was visiting a family somewhere in the Midwest. Over dinner, as was his pastoral duty, the priest reminded the family, and especially the children of the family, that God made all the good things on the earth. The priest then pointed to the refrigerator and said that even things stored in there came from Jehovah. 'Jehovah?' said one of the astonished children. 'But I thought Jehovah Menuhin was a violinist.'

But, as we have seen, it was the shock of war and its manifold injustices that focused Yehudi's institutional activities, first as a lobbyist for particular individuals, and later for matters of more general concern. It was his involvement with Russian musicians, moreover, and his increasing awareness of their difficulties under the Brezhnev regime, that brought the particular and the general together.

In October 1971, the biennial congress of the International Music Council, an affiliate of UNESCO, was due to be held in Moscow. The previous year, Yehudi had been unanimously elected president. For some time he had been trying to secure permission for David Oistrakh, the great Russian violinist, to visit Yehudi's new festival in Gstaad where the Menuhins had recently taken up residence. The Minister of Culture was still Khrushchev's daughter-in-law, the imperiously unpleasant Irina Furtseva. Yehudi's tireless criticism of Russian thuggery, whether the invasion of Czechoslovakia or the Soviet authorities' refusal to allow Jews to emigrate to Israel, had annoyed Madame Furtseva so much that she had been heard to say that she would never allow *any* Russian artist to play with the dreadful Menuhin. But even Furtseva was unwilling to risk the international disapproval of UNESCO, and to avoid further confrontation promised to send Igor Oistrakh, David's son and also an exceptional violinist, to Gstaad.

Yehudi was mollified, but already planning his counter-attack. Following his re-election as president (proposed by the Russians, who thus once again displayed their endless capacity for double-think), Yehudi strode on to the podium to deliver his presidential address. Although Russian in origin, his spoken Russian was poor. On this occasion, however, he had learned his entire speech in Russian (his memory has always been phenomenal), and began by praising Russian cultural achievements, whether in literature, music or painting. He did not advocate the free-market system of the West, he said: he did not particularly criticize what he knew to be the absurd restrictions on the professional lives of his fellow Russian musicians. But he did mention those Russian artists whom he admired: Shostakovich, who had been in and out of official favour so often that the psychological schizophrenia had almost destroyed him physically; Yevtushenko, who, in spite of his unofficial role as court jester, was in 1971 under a deep cloud of official disapproval;

and Solzhenitsyn, whose Nobel Prize awarded in 1970 had been violently attacked by Furtseva as merely the latest attempt by the West to discredit Russian art.

Not surprisingly, *Pravda* failed to mention a word of Yehudi's speech, although news of what he had said spread rapidly. According to Yehudi, he was frequently stopped in the street, in hotel corridors and backstage with a touch of the hand, 'a gift slipped into my pocket', or a 'whispered congratulation'. And so, armed with the feeling that he had touched a nerve in the Russian consciousness, Yehudi (the institution) decided to challenge the institution of the Russian state. Intending to plead for two particular individuals who wanted their families to join them in the West, Yehudi demanded an interview with the Ministry of Culture. Furtseva had by now conveniently 'left' Moscow; so had her immediate deputy. But Supagin, the number three with special responsibilities for visiting artists, agreed to see him.

The conversation was acrimonious. If the laws of the USSR were half as strict as the West maintained, Yehudi was told, Solzhenitsyn would be in prison. Every reply Yehudi made was described by Supagin as 'capitalist propaganda'. Stalin was invoked as hero and father of the Soviet people, and the West's obsession with drugs and violence as justification for 'not letting people do what they want to'. '*We*,' said Supagin, 'have great plans for them.' Yehudi stormed out, his patience exhausted.

The hostility of Russian officialdom to Yehudi continued for some years. Three years later, for instance, at a special twenty-fifth anniversary celebration of the IMC in Paris, the cellist Rostropovich mysteriously failed to show up. Oh, he's had a heart attack and cannot travel, Yehudi was told. Horrified, Yehudi managed to get hold of Rostropovich's wife, Galina Vishnevskaya, on the telephone. Rostropovich was in Georgia, giving a concert, she said. He'd been sent there by the Ministry. A heart attack? she asked in amusement. Who has told you this lie? Yehudi was furious and cabled the Ministry of Culture. No, Rostropovich was unavailable, but would Mr Menuhin accept Shostakovich and his new quartet as a substitute? (This must have been Shostakovich's 15th String Quartet, among his most bitter and personal attacks on the Soviet system. So the offer had an extraordinary irony and further demonstrated to Yehudi the total stupidity of the Ministry of Culture.) No, said Yehudi, he would accept no substitute and decided to cable Brezhnev himself, threatening to expose the lies the Ministry was telling. It is doubtful whether Brezhnev had ever heard of Menuhin; but Rostropovich got his visa and the Paris concert went ahead without further mishap.

To take on Russia in the sixties and seventies might have seemed fair game; the state of Israel was another matter, especially as Yehudi was Jewish. Perhaps it was inevitable that, like all Jewish artists of worldwide repute, Yehudi would sooner or later become involved publicly with the problems of Israel. After the Camp David agreement, for instance, it was the photograph of Yehudi playing before the Wailing Wall that did most to symbolize, internationally, the Egyptian/Israeli initiative. Not that Yehudi had any truck with Zionism, in the sense that Zionists claim the Jews have a *political* right to displace thousands, if not millions, of Palestinians and other Arabs because they believe the land of Israel belongs exclusively to them. Repeated attempts by Yehudi to persuade the Israeli leaders (notably Golda Meir) to consider the damage their wholesale resettlement of the Arabs was causing, fell on deaf ears. As Mrs Meir reminded him, *her* refugees were the displaced Jews of Russia, of Poland and of Germany. They had come to Israel 'to fulfil themselves, not to liberate others'.

Such an attitude, however understandable, was bound to irritate Yehudi. As we have seen, Yehudi's presidency of the International Music Council had pushed him further and further centre stage in the political arena. As part of UNESCO, itself part of the United Nations, the IMC was supposedly above politics. But when, for instance, the question of China's admission to the UN in the period immediately after President Nixon's China adventure had become politically important, it was suggested to the IMC that it might be expedient to expel Taiwan in the hope of persuading (or allowing) China to join. The IMC, at Yehudi's insistence, refused. Likewise when UNESCO had officially censured Israel in November 1974 for its occupation of the West Bank, for its desecration of Muslim holy places in Jerusalem and for its demolition of Arab houses to make way for the new Israeli townships, Yehudi convinced himself (and the IMC) that this was the kind of political involvement that was beyond the scope of either UNESCO or the IMC. He was shocked by an open letter published simultaneously in London, Paris and New York, and signed by over two hundred musicians (among them Leonard Bernstein and Isaac Stern), supporting the UNESCO resolution. In a letter of surprising toughness, Yehudi wrote to Bernstein urging moderation. Public condemnation of Israel, he argued, particularly in such a bellicose and chauvinistic manner, would only harden hearts, 'obscure the issue' and prevent dialogue. 'Every wise and courageous friend is a precious asset to Israel,' Yehudi wrote.

The naïvety of Yehudi's appeal had (and has) a certain attraction. It was said that he underestimated entirely a) the siege mentality of most Israelis; b) the fear (understandable) which most Israelis felt toward the Arabs; and c) the pig-headed nostalgia that even non-Zionists felt towards an ancient, almost mythical 'fatherland'. Yehudi's point was more simple, he argued. To criticize the Israelis for a policy born out of practical need and religious justification solved nothing. Dialogue was always preferable to confrontation, and never more so than when the quarrel was about a strip of land over which two different people both claimed sovereignty.

Nonetheless, ignoring – or rather refusing to make any concession to – what most people would want to call political reality, Yehudi Menuhin, a violinist, plunged on. He wrote to various political leaders in Israel demanding a meeting. He threatened to resign as president of the IMC. At the next gathering of the IMC (in Toronto,

September 1975), he proposed a Middle Eastern 'Federation of Cultures', comprising members from Egypt, Iraq, Syria, Tunisia and Israel. 'It's our solemn duty,' he told the delegates, 'to conduct ourselves in a way which can give comfort and hope to humanity at large ... as would befit the dignity and dedication of our calling.' And this was not a Kissinger or even a President Carter speaking. This was a man with no political power, a man of no real influence (even as president of the IMC) other than his perceived moral stature. Yehudi, the protected and apparently ignorant child from San Francisco, was now challenging the United Nations itself on one of the more contentious issues of the decade.

Some of his ideas were bizarre, such as suggesting to UNESCO that 'every parliament should have voices for the speechless, [and] deputies who represent the fowl of the air and the fish of the sea.' But his notion that *cultures* should have representation at international gatherings such as the UN is an important idea deserving better attention than it has hitherto received. Do the Red Indians of North America not deserve recognition? Or the Kurds? Or the Aborigines? Is it not true that the Ukrainians are quite different in culture from the Uzbekis? If so, why are they represented internationally by the same delegation from Moscow? 'Without losing loyalty to one's nation,' Yehudi told the IMC congress, 'our era demands of a newer, wider loyalty and allegiance.'

Such considerations have, I maintain, become more and more central to Yehudi's whole way of life; more so, perhaps, than his violin-playing. Partly this has come about because, in his innermost self, he has never regained that sublime innocence and trust in his playing that carried him to such astonishing heights of artistry when he was young. Partly his dream world of childhood and its aspirations have been tarnished (if not destroyed) by Nola and Belsen (dreams and images both), although one must be careful not to exaggerate their long-term effect. It is clear to me that Yehudi has often sought to reconstruct his world of dreams on a global scale; when challenged about the unreality of some of his ideas, he merely replies: 'Is it useless, or even worse than use-less, to try?'

He has been called a fascist for attempting to intervene in Greek politics after the overthrow of the military regime in 1974; he has been labelled a traitor (to Israel) because of his insistence on playing in post-Nazi Germany; he has also been called (by *The Times* of London) 'a man for all seasons', implying that because he played violin concertos, Indian ragas, jazz and chamber music as well as trying to run his own festival (at that time in Bath), he had begun to command little respect in any of these disciplines. Indeed, as his activities have increased in range and scope – as the critic Neville Cardus once remarked, 'Menuhin [has] learned to put his . . . beautiful range of colours at the service of his developing mind and musical insights. Only the second-rate remain static' – it has sometimes become difficult to know exactly who or what is Yehudi Menuhin.

Diana recalls being sent a copy of an IQ test for children which contained the question: 'Who or what is Yehudi Menuhin? Delete which is not applicable: a) a world-famous cyclist; b) a Chinese Emperor; c) a kind of Indian food; d) the patron saint of music.' In her hilarious – although not entirely accurate – description of their early life together entitled *Fiddler's Moll*, she admits that the definition which appealed to her most was the world-famous cyclist. After all, she says, Yehudi has put a girdle round the earth in what often feels like forty minutes almost every year of his life; so the idea of him as some kind of athlete on wheels is not quite as absurd as it might at first appear.

Even to his children Yehudi has become – in Krov's description – one of 'civilization's markers'. He is 'something, someone to aspire to,' Krov says. 'His sense of priorities, his skill as a violinist, but above all, his humility, mark him out.' '*Everything* Yehudi does,' Diana told me, 'is entirely and purely instinctive. And that is why one must sleep with one eye constantly open, because one never knows if his instincts are going to take him in the right direction or not. He never questions, and that's his main problem. But on the other hand you cannot say anything definite to him, such as *don't do so-and-so*. He doesn't like it, or he chooses not to hear it. You have to say something vague, something that *might* influence him and hope it will take seed.'

It would be misleading, moreover, to suggest that Yehudi never questions his new-found role. He has long since lost his childhood illusion that music was or is 'an irresistible force for good', especially as he has come to realize that by 'music' he meant Western music in general and nineteenth-century German music (or the tradition which it embodied) in particular. The moral values which others have ascribed to Bach or Beethoven, he says, would frequently have horrified the composers themselves, for whom the idea that music could express moral values, except in purely aesthetic terms, was anathema.

But Yehudi still believes in what he would inadequately describe as the 'eternal' values of music. Against these values he sees his own attempts to intervene on the world's political stage as little more than 'an amiable fool blundering into delicate situations', or as a 'self-righteous prig who believes everyone else is marching out of step'; at best, he is a man who 'pits conviction against received opinion'. 'But nothing has taught me to believe,' he replies in his autobiography, 'that music must be weak before human implaca-bility ... [or that] the wise musician should dumbly fiddle while the world burns.'

While writing this last sentence, I was telephoned by one of Yehudi's sons. After pleasantries, I asked if he had seen his father recently, and if so, where. Oh yes, said the son, I saw him last week in Switzerland. At a concert? I enquired. Oh no, said the son, without a tinge of criticism, let alone sarcasm. He was in Switzerland trying to save the Alps! (Recently, even the Swiss have become environmentally conscious, and been made aware that the endless new ski slopes and ski lifts are radically changing one of Switzerland's most valuable assets, namely its countryside. Inevitably, it was Yehudi, a violinist, who had turned up '... to save the Alps!')

This exchange then reminded me of an early-morning phone call I had had from Yehudi when I had almost completed my film portrait of him. He asked me how finished the film was, and how it was shaping up. Sensing there must be a corollary to this apparently innocent question, I muttered something about no film ever being truly finished, although in fact the Menuhin film had long since been completed. 'Oh good,' he said. 'I'm so glad it's not absolutely finished, because I have a small idea which I think we should include, and which I know will alter the whole balance of our work together.' Believing this was to be another revelation about his childhood or something of equal importance, I agreed to meet him later that day to discuss it.

Over tea he produced from his pocket a battered proof of a book about to be published concerning the encroaching Sahara desert in northern Nigeria. There was one very dedicated scientist, Yehudi told me, who had settled on the edge of the Sahara and was conducting 'fascinating experiments' in tree and shrub growth which, the scientist believed, would halt and eventually reverse the tide of sand. 'Ah,' I said. 'And how does this concern our film?' 'But it's the centrepiece,' said Yehudi, positively bubbling with childlike enthusiasm. 'We should go immediately to the southern Sahara and film this man's work. With your film and my worldwide contacts,' Yehudi said, 'we can save the Sahara.' 'There is nothing I would like better,' I told him, 'than to save the Sahara.' Making polite excuses, I left. For some weeks I heard nothing further, and avoided telephoning Yehudi in case he misinterpreted my call as support for this bizarre expedition. Three months later I read in a newspaper that the 'world-famous violinist Yehudi Menuhin is to address an international group of geologists on the need to find solutions to the deforestation and devastation of Central Africa, from Ethiopia to northern Nigeria'.

In 1972, Yehudi published a book entitled *Themes and Variations*, a collection of his essays and lectures already printed in magazines as varied as *Punch* and *Music Magazine*, or else delivered to such as

UNESCO, the Royal Society or the BBC. The range of subject matter is bewildering, demonstrating both the breadth of his concerns and the extent to which audiences the world over were/are prepared to listen to him. Can this be true, to such a degree, of any other living musician?

To the British Architectural Association, he lectured on 'Architecture Today'; with an assembly of Indian politicians and intellectuals he discussed 'Cultural Influences of Empire'; to the Royal Society he lectured on 'Art and Science' as related concepts; to Bristol University he spoke on 'Complete Education', delivering a discourse on free will, totalitarianism, holiness, the physical ideal of beauty as expressed by the Greeks, the family and the nature of humour. Town planning; medicine and its misuse; liberty and obedience; the philosophical implications of self-sacrifice (including suicide) – such are the topics on which Yehudi is now expected to pronounce, and does so if this volume is a guide.

An essay on 'Heaven on Earth' inevitably deals with the environment, a fashionable enough subject in 1990, yet Yehudi was campaigning hard thirty years earlier. 'Must short-term finance always dictate to us?' he asks. Conservation is the defence of humanity. 'Man today has created as vicious and vindictive a God as ever extorted the tribute of a superstitious people. The dragon we worship enshrines the inanimate and consumes the animate.' Architecture today has 'as little regard for humanity as for battery hens'. We are in danger of 'becoming asphyxiated and suffocated with our own debris'. *Pace* Prince Charles, but Yehudi was already on the warpath in 1967, when no one gave tuppence for the wholesale destruction of our inner cities in the name of progress. Likewise a 'common home of Europe', which was a concept espoused by Yehudi twenty years before Mr Gorbachev found its advocacy convenient.

It is easy enough to mock Yehudi's global conscience – saving the Alps, and so forth. And when one is given (by Diana) the fifteen closely typed pages of organizations of which Yehudi is the founder, patron, executive president, or merely just a member of the council, one naturally assumes it is impossible for one man, let alone a violinist, to undertake all these activities with any thoroughness. Everything from the Blue Cross of India to the British Butterfly Conservation Society; from the Campaign against Psychiatric Abuses, to the Chinese Welfare Fund for the Handicapped; from the Haringey Anti-Fluoridation Group, to the International Solar Energy Committee; from the Jewish Braille Institute of America, to the National Pure Water Association; from the Sunshine Fund for Blind Babies, to the Justice for Tibet International.

Yet for each and every one of these organizations, Yehudi is a key figure. A source of inspiration, respectability and money; an indispensable focus of the world's attention; a man who commands the ear of politician and plutocrat alike; a man whose public prestige seems to have increased in inverse proportion to his prowess as a violinist; a man whom music nearly destroyed; a man for whom, eventually, music was not enough. The transformation from Musician to Institution is a crucial step in trying to understand that Yehudi has become more than a world-famous cyclist.

7

The Musician

'Yehudi had often said to me,' Diana recalled, 'that not everybody has the luck to be born of Jewish parents who give up their lives for their son. Well, leaving aside whether, ultimately, it was lucky or not,' she went on, 'I suddenly realized that here was a way to *restore* his musical health, to show him, to allow him to feel that the violin was his friend again, and that the violin wasn't his *only* friend. If he were able to have a *school*, for instance, to encourage and help the young in the way that he felt *he* had been encouraged, then maybe he could rediscover his past in a way that would allow him to understand the present and contemplate the future with some equanimity.'

It was during Yehudi's first visit to the Soviet Union in November 1945, and in particular to the Central School of Music in Moscow, that the idea for a similar institution in the West had first occurred to him. After rigorous auditions, the Russian children were accepted aged five and then educated until sixteen. The courses were predominantly, although not exclusively, musical, and no child was allowed to perform in public outside the confines of the school. Thus, as Yehudi noted without a touch of irony, child prodigies were unknown in Russia. At sixteen, the most gifted children continued their studies at the Moscow Conservatory, which was almost next door, until they were ready to launch themselves on an astonished public in their early twenties. Not surprisingly, competition within the school was fierce, with pupils only being allowed to progress to stage two of their education after stage one had been completely mastered.

In the early sixties, after the Menuhins had taken up residence in London, Yehudi's long-time accompanist Marcel Gazelle and a brilliant ex-pupil Alberto Lysy were despatched to Moscow to learn what they could of the Central School and its methods. Plans were already fully underway for a Yehudi Menuhin School of Music to be founded on a fifteen-acre estate south of London at Stoke d'Abernon. The translation of the original idea into reality had actually begun in April 1961 with the formation of a Music Academy Committee, comprising the philanthropist Sir Robert Mayer and Ernest Reed, both passionately involved in music for children, Yehudi's lawyer and accountant, as well as the redoubtable figure of Ruth, Lady Fermoy, lady-in-waiting to the Queen Mother and grandmother of the future Princess Diana. Benefactors were persuaded (Yehudi has never had any problems finding benefactors) and at least *this* scheme had the advantage of being nearer to home and did not involve saving the Alps or the Sahara. Potential students were soon auditioned, and temporary accommodation found in Kensington, courtesy of the Arts Educational Trust.

Thus, eleven pupils, three teachers and a headmaster (Antony Brackenbury, an ex-master from Bryanston, one of England's more notable public schools) began work in September 1963. Like many of Yehudi's ideas, it was crazy, ill-prepared, trusting more to luck than judgement, but it worked. Within a year, the school had decamped to Stoke d'Abernon (where it still is), a financial trust organized to administer the finances, auctions of works by famous contemporary artists such as Henry Moore, Chagall, Miró, Epstein and Kokoschka held to raise capital, the number of pupils increased to thirty-three, the resident staff to six, and an old barn transformed into a three-hundred-seat concert hall for the public.

If I make it seem as if the Yehudi Menuhin School happened more or less overnight, this is probably because of the way Yehudi relates the school's foundation, with such a burst of enthusiasm and pride that it is difficult not to get swept away in that same enthusiasm. While not on the scale of the Juilliard School in New York or the Royal College of Music in London, Yehudi's school has undoubtedly benefited from the pervading influence (and interests) of its founder; as Yehudi himself puts it, the school has been 'blessed by the influence of many minds and energies'. Ravi Shankar has taught there; so have Itzhak Perlman and Victoria Posnikova and Stéphane Grappelli; so have Louis Kentner, Yehudi's brother-in-law, and Nadia Boulanger. Most come out of affection for Yehudi; an invitation from Yehudi is, after all, almost impossible to refuse.

The permanent staff has been equally distinguished, if less famous: teachers such as Robert Masters, Jacqueline Gazelle, George Malcolm, Peter Norris and Barbara Kerslake. Today the school is financially secure thanks to contributions from three considerable foundations, the Gulbenkian, the Wolfson and the Lord Rayne Trust, although in its early days it depended for its security to an uncomfortable extent on Yehudi's earning capacity. He was once heard to remark that the school had almost ruined him financially. The school orchestra has performed in Washington for the President of the United States, in Windsor for the Queen of England, in Switzerland and in the Far East, as well as regularly in England. It now receives government bursaries although it is not mentioned in the government's official list of musical education establishments. But it exists, and is now the principal music school in Britain to which most young violinists aspire. (Nigel Kennedy was a pupil.) Its waiting list for entry is enormous.

Paradoxically, Yehudi ensured from the start that his pupils were not to be trained simply as virtuosi. Only four instruments are taught, violin, viola, cello and piano. Playing in chamber groups is encouraged, and the idea of a 'Menuhin method' (as, for instance, a 'Suzuki method') is actively discouraged simply because there is no 'Menuhin method'. Ironically, he admits that while the mysteries of his own precocious talent have become for him ever more inexplicable, no amount of contact with the talented children of his school has enlightened him. What began in both his own childhood and his ambitions for his pupils as a 'vision of the good and beautiful', has now become in the light of his experiences running the school 'uncomfortably indistinct'.

He writes movingly in his autobiography of early attempts at the school to prevent his pupils falling into the bad habits which he believes bedevilled his own development and finally unwound the springs of his own abilities. Don't grip the violin as if you were rivetted to it; allow the head and the neck of both pupil and violin to move freely; learn to breathe properly while playing, inhaling on an up-bow, exhaling on a down-bow; allow the elbow of the right arm to 'dangle' so that it is relaxed and supple.

Yehudi would admit that his school has different aims from, for example, that of the Japanese teacher Suzuki, which produce violinists of reasonable proficiency by the wagonload. And he eschews those violin (or viola, cello and piano) methodologies which never allow the pupil to reach beyond the simplest of exercises or the simplest of repertoire until love of violin, let alone love of music, has been well and truly killed off. It's almost as if he wants each pupil to attempt the Beethoven Violin Concerto as soon as he or she can make a noise marginally more than tolerable. 'I remember watching with pity a poor child walking along the street in San Francisco,' Yehudi told me, 'clutching a violin case as if he were walking to the condemned cell. So when I began my school, I vowed that this would never be so. My school is for ordinary children who are musically gifted and who need to be given a chance. When I see them in concert, unselfconsciously full of life, affirming the joy of music and finding fulfilment as I did, I have vindication enough. Apart from anything else, it proves to me that I have been normal all along!' Or, as Diana puts it, the school has helped Yehudi to accept once again that the violin is his friend.

I shall return later to the question of Yehudi's place in musical history. But one of the unanswered questions in Yehudi's musical life is how one of the most famous violinists of our time does not, in performance now, receive the respect (not affection, but respect – a crucial difference) among fellow musicians that his reputation ought to command. Certainly, there is no denying that a solo performance by Menuhin today can sometimes be an ordeal. Notes are missing; intonation is wobbly; the pressure on the bow as it passes across the strings is so unsure that often unusual noises result – squeaks, pops and thuds. And what can be even more embarrassing is the realization that Menuhin himself seems totally unaware of what is happening. A 1985 performance of the second movement of the Beethoven Concerto, with the Moscow Philharmonic conducted by Gennadi Rozhdesvensky, exists on film. The vibrato is out of control, the harmonics are screeches, the scales are unworthy of a pupil at Yehudi's school. But Rozhdesvensky remains unperturbed; the orchestra plays on as if nothing unusual is happening; and little registers on Yehudi's face (except sublime concentration) to indicate anything less than perfection. Is he unaware? Equally, why are *we* fascinated, even mesmerized? Why do we go on calling him a 'great violinist'? Is it simply in grateful memory of those early, remarkable recordings? Is it an unwillingness to see one of our heroes destroyed? Is it disbelief that this can be happening at all? Diana sometimes blames his poor playing on mean-minded critics (an attractive option), and always cites one 'particularly obnoxious fellow' who had the temerity to suggest, after a performance of the Beethoven Concerto, that it was about time Menuhin put away his violin for good.

In 1987, EMI, the recording label for whom Yehudi had worked for over fifty years, did not wish to renew his contract in the terms being offered. Yehudi's manager was understandably shocked. Arguing that Yehudi 'no longer wished to play as much as he did', she had tried to persuade EMI to continue Yehudi's contract principally in terms of his 'new' career, that of a conductor. After all, she argued, EMI had made a small fortune from the immense catalogue of Yehudi's recordings which continued to outsell many younger and more contemporary names. Surely EMI owed Yehudi the benefit of the doubt over Yehudi's 'new' career? EMI hesitated. They had enough conductors, they said.

Sensing that this rejection might deal a fatal blow not just to Yehudi's pride but also to his general well-being – music was, after all, his life – the manager lighted upon one of the more enterprising of the new recording labels, Virgin Classics. A contract was agreed which provided for Yehudi to deliver a minimum number of new records (CDs) per year over five years, with Yehudi conducting. The first of these recordings took place in Warsaw in January 1989, the repertoire being predominantly Mozart symphonies. Yehudi thereby renewed his partnership with the Warsaw Sinfonia, one of the finest chamber ensembles in Europe.

Prior to these recordings, I had seen Yehudi at work with the Warsaw Sinfonia in Vienna for a performance of Handel's *Messiah* (in the Mozart arrangement); thence with the Staatskapelle in Dresden at a concert to celebrate the sixtieth anniversary of Yehudi's first appearance in Dresden in 1929. In a break during rehearsals, Yehudi told me that he had first taken up the conductor's baton at the suggestion of Antal Dorati, the Hungarian maestro, as long ago as 1942. (It was also Dorati who had urged Yehudi to discover the music of Bartók.) 'Dorati simply stood me in front of his orchestra in Dallas,' Yehudi said, 'put a baton in my hand and said, "Go ahead. It's the *Meistersinger* overture." I had barely raised my trembling hand when I heard this huge C major chord and realized that *they* had made the noise, not *I*. And of course I tripped on the conductor's podium and was saved by the first violinist! I'm sure he thought of me more as one of them, than as a conductor!'

The rehearsals in both Dresden and Vienna were, from a musical point of view, a shambles – yet utterly fascinating. Yehudi's conducting technique, for instance, his ability to convey a clear beat which the orchestra can follow, is, to put it mildly, haphazard. This in itself is not necessarily a disadvantage. Furtwängler's baton quivered to such an extent, and his head wobbled to such a degree, that his whole body often resembled a jellyfish in shock; Karajan managed to convey nuance with a twitch of the left eyebrow. By contrast, conductors with a rigid beat often produce music which is dead from the neck down.

But Yehudi's apparent musical ignorance was more surprising. The music of Handel, even when smoothed out by Mozart, derives much of its vigour from precise rhythm and precise ornamentation. The ornamentation (often including rhythmic variation) can be deviously subtle, and depends partly on the skill of the performers, partly on the knowledge of the conductor, and partly on the freedom which he (or she) allows the players and soloists. Even if Yehudi *knew* the rhythms and ornamentation which are now central to any authentic performance of Handel, he rehearsed the Hallelujah Chorus (for example) with such heaviness that no subtlety was possible. The orchestra struggled to follow his beat, occasionally missing an entry altogether through Yehudi's misdirection; the choir (the Vienna State Opera Chorus) plodded on regardless, as lumpen and as dangerous to health as most Austrian cream cakes.

And yet, in discussion subsequently with various members of the orchestra, there was little doubt that Yehudi was among their favourite conductors. The inadequacies of his technique mattered little to them, and of Yehudi's poor (not to say anachronistic) knowledge of early eighteenth-century music, they cared even less. What he imparted to them, they said, was first a sense of tradition, of continuity in music-making. Here was a direct link back to Toscanini, to Busch, to Elgar, to Bartók, to Furtwängler. Second, here was a man who went straight to the heart of a piece of music, almost straight to the heart of the composer himself; who knew, even if only instinctively, what the music was about, which was after all more than a collection of black dots upon a printed page, more than a knowledge of ornamentation, more than a personal whim as to tempo or phrasing. Here, members of the orchestra told me, was no attempt at personal interpretation, no attempt at self-aggrandizement at the expense of the music. Here, instead, was a medium through which the composer spoke, directly but unmistakably. Like Stravinsky when describing the composition of *The Rite of Spring*, Menuhin could truly say that he was a vessel through which the music flowed.

An even more absorbing illustration of this process occurred in the newly rebuilt Semper Opera House in Dresden. Yehudi was rehearsing Mozart's Symphony No. 41, 'the 'Jupiter', a notoriously difficult piece. Like all Mozart, the music appears so deceptively simple, so elegant, so easy to play from a technical point of view; in fact, it is infinitely elusive, its spirit forever slipping through one's fingers like sand. Bad or indifferent performances of the 41st Symphony far outnumber adequate, let alone good, performances. Stunning performances are as rare as Shakespeare's signature.

At the rehearsal, Yehudi plunged without hesitation into the first movement. The tempo was fast, anxious, urgent, full of menace. It was almost as if Yehudi had not previously considered the tempo, merely responded in his imagination to performances heard long ago and echoing now in his memory. The players (Dresden Staatskapelle) responded to the challenge magnificently, with tension and with furious passion, as if they too were discovering the music for the first time. Certainly they can never have played it before at such a lick. The climaxes were exhilarating; one's hair rose on the back of one's neck; one's hands were suddenly sweaty; one's pulse noticeably began to race. Yehudi got lost, and at one point seemed to be conducting an entirely different piece. But the orchestra had been unleashed, and, like the great chamber ensemble they are, careered away in perfect control yet with a wild abandon I have rarely heard.

When the first movement came to an end, the orchestra instantly burst into chatter; heads nodded at one another in bewildered recognition of what had just happened. Yehudi was exhausted. Finally he said: 'Maybe the tempo was a little fast, but . . .' whereupon the entire orchestra applauded him. It had been a moment of music-making which I am sure none of them will ever forget; any more than a hundred, a thousand other similar occasions when

Yehudi's gift has manifested itself in this miraculous and unpredictable way.

I believe that Yehudi is frightened by this gift, in much the same way as many creative artists are overawed by what it is they create, reluctant to believe that an ordinary human being can be responsible for such things, such moments of insight; preferring to believe that only divine inspiration can accept such responsibility, while knowing this to be unlikely. 'My conducting career has been charmingly topsy-turvy,' Yehudi writes in his autobiography.

He might also have written that his recording career has been charmingly topsy-turvy. Apart from any other considerations, there can be few musicians whose recording career has lasted over sixty years. Not even von Karajan could emulate that. From Yehudi's earliest recording with Louis Persinger – recorded, mastered, processed and in the shops within twenty-four hours – to his latest CDs with Virgin Classics, he has always championed new works and music not in the standard repertoire. In all, Yehudi has made over four hundred records, with combined sales in excess of twenty million units. He was the first to record Berlioz's *Harold in Italy*, the Bartók Viola Concerto, and the symphonies of William Boyce. His recordings of the Bach solo violin sonatas were the first to bring this exceptional music to a wide public. Aged sixty, he made a list of all those pieces which he still intended to record. There was enough work (as he modestly put it) to keep him going for several decades.

This sublimation of self reached its apotheosis in the various music festivals with which Yehudi became associated. Most musicians who begin festivals in their name, or in their own image, do so primarily to promote their own work; Wagner at Bayreuth; Menotti at Spoleto; even Benjamin Britten at Aldeburgh. In 1959, at the suggestion of his then British manager, Ian Hunter, Yehudi became artistic director of the Bath Festival. 'Once again I put my family, my friends and my past to use,' he told me.

More importantly, the festivals again provided him with a musical security which his concert career had of late begun to undermine. Already the reviewers were becoming less than charitable. He pretended he didn't notice; Diana would claim he didn't even read what was being written. But in so far as he deliberately tried to recreate the same atmosphere he believed had existed in his childhood – when 'my two sisters provided all I ever needed' – it seems that in throwing himself into the organization of the Bath Festival (for instance), Yehudi was perhaps seeking refuge from his anxiety that something was wrong. Both sisters performed regularly in Bath; as did both brothers-in-law; as did his son-in-law. His ten-year-old son now played the piano; his wife read poetry; he conducted his ex-pupils, the local youth orchestra and his school. Friends came: Shankar, Oistrakh, Nadia Boulanger. With Robert Masters, the musical director of his school, Yehudi founded the Bath Festival Orchestra, which he conducted and with which he made famous recordings of the Mozart violin concertos. Again, there are wrong notes, but the playing is as delicate and tragic and wistful as only Mozart can be, and as only Yehudi (among very few others) can achieve.

I'm not saying that in Bath little music of any consequence occurred. Quite the contrary. The duets with Shankar, the 'jazz fusions' with the John Dankworth Orchestra, the visits by the Moscow Chamber Orchestra under Barshai, the first flowerings of the Fonteyn–Nureyev partnership, these were all memorable and notable performances. Peter Maxwell Davies, then still music master at Cirencester Grammar School, gave first performances of his work; Menotti brought an opera, *Martin's Lie*; Alexander Goehr premièred his Piano Trio; the cellist Jacqueline du Pré began her international career at Bath thanks to Yehudi's advocacy of her skills; George Szell conducted almost his last concert in England, Pierre Boulez almost his first; Yehudi himself gave what most critics at the time agreed was the definitive version of the Berg Violin Concerto. And meanwhile Yehudi was busy saving the Abbey, organizing campaigns to clean up the canals near Bath, and objecting to various hideous new buildings which the Bath City Council was threatening to put up.

But the Bath Festival never rivalled Salzburg or Edinburgh, never became an essential place of pilgrimage for the discerning music lover, never was more than a comfortable, bourgeois get-together for the local gentry (and their children). If this is cruel, it has to be remembered that the Bath Festival under Yehudi existed at a time (the mid-sixties) when European youth and culture were in turmoil. Revolution was on everyone's lips, except, it seems, in Bath.

And when the Menuhin caravan moved on to Windsor in 1969 (again with Ian Hunter), it was as if England and English music-making as exemplified by Yehudi had completely failed to notice the momentous changes which were happening around them. The Queen lived at Windsor, and the Queen gave Yehudi a farewell party when, after three years, he finally tired of being responsible for the festival. 'It was a lovely party in a lovely place,' Yehudi wrote later. The Queen invited 'those typically British figures in public life, as well as the military who are born musicians, painters and poets'. It had been a long journey from Belsen.

In Gstaad, where Yehudi had finally settled in the mid-fifties, a similar pattern emerged. Begun in 1956 (and still continuing), the festival soon became the ski resort's answer to what to do in the summer months. Held mostly in the parish church of the neighbouring community of Saanen (an exquisite sixteenth-century galleried building), the four week music get-together has also seen some remarkable events. As I said, who can resist an invitation from Yehudi? And if the music-making has often centred around the same group of friends or pupils that also featured in Bath or Windsor, the friends were, after all, some of the leading musicians of the day. If no attempt has been made to give the festival a distinctive, even unique, character – such as 'contemporary music' at Donaueschingen, or 'mostly Mozart' at Salzburg – it does satisfy the local Swiss community as well as Yehudi's international audience, and it does (as we shall see) provide an opportunity for the Menuhin family to gather at Gstaad for their annual reunion.

Conditions in the church at Saanen are a little primitive. The dressing area for the artists is a tiny upstairs loft, not big enough to swing a cat without clobbering all present. But Yehudi happily mingles with the visiting soloists who are sometimes dismayed by the lack of space; hardly room to unpack in, let alone practise; and by the time wives, girlfriends and the ever-present church warden have crowded in, no space to breathe. On such occasions, Yehudi seems to crouch in a corner, sipping tea from a flask always provided by Diana, who usually appears at the last moment jabbering away in French, English and German, all fluently and often (it seems) simultaneously, while trying to comb the maestro's hair. Well, 'at least there's less and less hair as the years go by,' she tells him. 'Yes darling,' he replies.

Yehudi, the day of a concert, whether conducting or performing, is a strange sight. After sixty years on the road it is not surprising that he has perfected a very orderly routine. If he is committed to a solo recital, for instance, the following rules apply: Do not visit the concert hall the day of performance. Rather, spend the time sleeping and exercising. A violinist, he told me, is constantly in training since 'the violinist's body must vibrate just as the violin does.' Posture is essential. Thus, practice (on the violin) begins with Yehudi lying on his back. He raises both arms, then both legs, separately, then together. He rotates them. Then, he 'lets them dangle'. He 'checks each joint, and feels its individual weight'.

Breathing exercises come next, coordinating the movements of the limbs with the inhaling and exhaling of breath. The whole body must become as 'supple as a reed', able to 'catch motion on the wing'. Nothing is worse, Yehudi told me, than a violinist who is stiff, as if the violin were fixed to the violinist or the violinist fixed to the violin. The delicacy with which the violin bow must touch the strings is such that the merest stiffness can ruin the sound. Worse, as the pressure required on one string is not the same as on another, the bowing arm must always be 'in sympathy' with this pressure.

The body must become an 'aural intelligence', and as such will require the appropriate diet. As a child, Yehudi was fed raw fruit and vegetables by Marutha. She never allowed him sweets or anything fried. Canned food was forbidden. Salads were essential. 'In company,' Yehudi admits, 'I occasionally succumb to fish.' At his school, white flour and white sugar are discouraged.

On tour he carries with him what seems like a cabinet full of bottles containing a variety of multi-coloured pills, of which he says the most important is a decoction of powdered yeast, vitamins and honey. For Yehudi, urination, defecation, as well as simple digestion, are subjects of vital importance, and likely to be dropped into the conversation without warning. After all, he says with a smile, they are the crucial processes of life, the basic functions of our bodies. If we cannot understand these, and take steps to ensure they occur normally, what chance do we have of training our bodies to achieve anything else?

In a lecture delivered at the 1962 Dartington Hall Summer School of Music in Devon, southwest England, Yehudi developed his theory about violin-playing to almost mystical proportions. 'To play the violin,' he said, 'it is necessary to form clear images of the interaction of four distinct directions, which parallel the four directions in the global circle.' Horizontal push and pull; weight from above; and weight from below. In other words, a delicate interplay between weight, balance and motion. Violin-playing is 'a series of half-circles, embodying both the static principles of the arch, as in a bridge, and the dynamic principles of motion as exemplified by the pendulum'. And, to make his point abundantly clear, Yehudi added that violin-playing is *also* 'a series of whole circles . . . embodying the static, structural self-supporting principles of a sphere, and the dynamic one of a wheel in motion'.

The violinist, after all, must be self-supporting. He has no instrument to rest on, like a piano; no external support, like a cello. From the very start, Yehudi says, a violinist must learn 'to float and carry; to drift with the stream of motion or emotion'. Failure to do so will result in 'a folding back of the body and mind upon itself', the inevitable consequence of which is 'sickness and pain'. The 'conflict of opposing muscles must be resolved', so that a 'giving-out of oneself, an embracing of as wide a world as possible' will result. This 'giving-out of oneself' is also called Love. Thus, in violin-playing, the practical and the philosophical must advance hand in hand.

It is tempting to dismiss such theorizing as mumbo-jumbo. And while there is no doubt that Yehudi's belief is genuine, there is equally no doubt that he was ignorant of any such theory when he began playing so magically as a boy. In his relentless pursuit of an explanation for this magic, he had led himself down many a by-way. He himself often says that music has no need of verbal explanation, and maybe he should have followed his own advice. Nonetheless, one is reminded of a true story told about an admirer of Paganini. This admirer was so desperate to learn the secret of Paganini's virtuosity that he followed the great violinist throughout one of his many tours, even camping outside his hotel bedroom and constantly peering through the keyhole hoping to observe the legendary figure when he practised. To the increasing dismay of the admirer, however, Paganini never seemed to practise, or if he did it was never at a time when the admirer could catch him. Then, one day, to his surprise and delight, the admirer saw Paganini open the violin case and put the violin to his chin. At last, thought the admirer, I shall learn the secret. But after a few moments of some-what desultory playing, Paganini replaced the violin in its case and that was that. Frustrated beyond endurance, the admirer burst into Paganini's room, and demanded to know when and where the maestro practised, and if not why not, and what had he achieved by the two or three phrases the admirer had witnessed seconds before. Paganini smiled and said simply that what he had just done was all he ever needed to do. 'I only needed to reassure myself,'

Paganini said, 'that my mind and body remain securely integrated.
The rest is mere fingerwork.'

I suspect that Yehudi sometimes follows the implications of this
dictum to unfortunate absurdity, giving himself an excuse for not
practising – or, at least, not as much as he should. The story also
provides Yehudi with an explanation for those days on which his
technique is less than secure. The mind and the body were not
working together as well as they should, he can say. His ambition
to become like a 'Zen archer, so self-aware that he will hit his target
blindfold' is admirable, but, since he is not yet in a state of grace,
inadequate. One problem is that Yehudi occasionally confuses the
mystical nature of music itself with his own (equally mysterious)
skill on the violin. It is no coincidence, Yehudi explains, that Einstein
was a violinist. '"Time" is no mere abstraction to a musician,' he
says. Rather, it is 'an infinite, living, pulsating continuum, varied
and mobile ... its laws identical with those interacting ones of
gravity, speed and weight which govern spatial phenomena'. The
Greeks, after all, 'found music in the heavenly spheres'.

Music removes us from reality, Yehudi argues, while at the same
time confronting us with a reality more unnerving than that from
which we believe we have escaped. Music is a clue to the personality
of a people, of a time and of a creator. Music is order out of
chaos. Through music we share in each other's sorrow, exhilaration,
solitude and peace. Music is a house of worship, a silent confessional,
a call to arms, a riverbed whose flow charts our subterranean levels
of consciousness. All of these aphorisms – and a hundred more –
one finds littered about Yehudi's writings. Again it is impossible to
question the sincerity of his belief in them; but, like many aphorisms, they are often used as an excuse for disciplined and rational
thought. In Yehudi's case, it is ironic that they have occurred with
greater and greater frequency the more he has been called upon to
pronounce about the evils of the world. If he is expected to speak
up on architecture, or science, or the environment, or on behalf of
homes for old tired bicycles, why should he not pronounce about

that which is his profession, music? However, most of his more discerning admirers (*pace* Paganini) would willingly sacrifice ten thousand words for an hour of his playing as once it was.

There are, of course, numerous musical topics on which he has been both eloquent and influential. First, like most performing artists, he is particularly sensitive to the acoustics of a hall that he has to perform in. He has campaigned tirelessly against architects and engineers who have built concert halls which are 'aesthetically pleasing', but in which 'even an elephant would have a problem being properly heard'. The Royal Festival Hall in London, he says, is dead; like an operating theatre, wherein the lights 'cast no shadow, allow no depth, configuration or perspective'. Yehudi played there with Hephzibah the day after the official opening in 1951. The stage was so low, Yehudi complained, that it was 'calculated to reduce a concert to a street incident'. As to its sister hall, the Queen Elizabeth, the royal adjective (according to Yehudi) merely describes the nature of the tomb.

When Lincoln Center was being built in New York in the early sixties, he tried to persuade the sponsors to emulate and imitate some of the great concert halls of Europe, both in terms of the proposed height and depth of the building, as well as the kinds of material from which it was to be constructed. All to no avail. The 'concrete bunker' which resulted (the Avery Fisher Hall) had to be rebuilt (several times) at a cost of several million dollars, before any major soloist could play there with any satisfaction. By comparison, Yehudi told me, the standard wooden US Army barracks which he had frequented during the war were bliss. 'A recital in a tunnel,' on the other hand (Avery Fisher Hall?), is like 'swimming against a tide of molten toffee'.

Second, there is Yehudi's constant advocacy of the value of a musical education for the young, epecially for those not destined to become part of the profession. And I am not speaking here about his school. Yehudi's friendship with Bartók, and later Kodaly, took him (as we have seen) to Hungary after the war, where he was amazed to learn that in most Hungarian schools the day began with each class singing unaccompanied choruses, often by Kodaly and usually for at least one hour. Carl Orff, the German composer of *Carmina Burana*, was attempting to secure much the same discipline in the schools of the Federal Republic, the idea being that the children were literally 'toned up' by this routine, with their 'spiritual, intellectual and psychological capacities' stretched and invigorated as a result.

Yehudi's attempts to introduce the Kodaly method (or similar) into the various schools under the control of the then Greater London Council alas came to nothing. But Yehudi remains Patron of the European Community Youth Orchestra, Patron of the National Youth Choir of Great Britain, as well as Vice-President of 'Youth and Music'.

And if his school has satisfied or fulfilled what he perceives as his obligations to those less fortunate than himself – 'not all children have two devoted Jewish parents' – then his writings about music have also in part satisfied or fulfilled the debt he has felt towards his fellow musicians, a debt he could no longer repay entirely through his playing. 'My life has been spent in trying to create Utopia,' he wrote once. But, as he admitted, this ambition was bound to fail, and has been constantly modified into an attempt to 'mould reality into something that justifies happiness'. Has *this* been his achievement as a musician over the last sixty years?

The difficulty in attempting any assessment of Yehudi as a musician is contained in that question. Today it is fashionable to discount Yehudi as a violinist, let alone a conductor. Few great conductors have played with him in the last few years, and he rarely performs with any conductor who is not an old friend or a beginner, neither of whom would wish to make Yehudi feel uncomfortable.

Yet the reaction in the past of fellow musicians and great conductors is undeniable. Furtwängler described Yehudi's playing as a 'beatitude', a 'blessing'. Neville Cardus, the critic, said that Yehudi had been born 'great'. Because he had been born of Russian Jewish parents, he had become a violinist. Had he been born of other parents, he might have become a 'great' poet, or a 'great' philosopher. The first occasion on which Zubin Mehta, the Indian-born conductor of the Los Angeles Philharmonic, played with Yehudi, he admitted he had previously been a little doubtful. After the first rehearsal, however, he told Diana that he had completely forgotten what it was to play with a 'communicator'. Piatigorsky, the cellist, once challenged Yehudi to play a new and particularly difficult trio, and was astonished to discover not merely that Yehudi could sight-read more or less all of the notes more or less in the right order, but that he 'played the music as if he had been playing it all his life'. The young British cellist Robert Cohen told me the same. He remembered a first rehearsal of a Brahms trio which was a little difficult. Yehudi had made many mistakes – of intonation, phrasing and bowing – in a work he must have known since childhood. At a second rehearsal, however, it was not so much that all the notes were now more or less correct, but that Yehudi's grasp of the essential spirit of the music was so profound that Cohen left the rehearsal shaken by his own lack of understanding.

For Yehudi, as for all great violinists, his instrument is alive in a way that, for instance, a piano is not. A piano responds to the pianist's most delicate intentions, Yehudi explained to me, but its mechanics 'strip [the notes] of vocal embellishments. A piano has the quality of a mechanical virgin, whereas a violin ... So I never play the violin,' he told me, 'without feeling that I have released violated spirits ... as if the wood itself stored its history and its soul.' Yehudi believes that the violin is his ultimate confessional, enabling him to make an intensely private apologia for his inadequacies, a meditation on his most secret troubles. If so, no wonder his playing changed after his broken marriage and his awful glimpse of man's inhumanity at Belsen. There can have been few performing musicians for whom their instrument has become so intimately an extension of their being. Yehudi usually describes his relationship with the various Stradivarii and Guarnerii which he has owned or played in personal terms, often as love affairs.

As to his Khevenhüller Stradivarius, Yehudi thought of it as his mistress. 'There was no winning her,' he says, 'except by incessant victories over oneself, by demonstrations of perfect control.' When he had not played it/her for a while, 'I found we must make each other's acquaintance again. It took a couple of weeks to become accustomed to one another,' to re-establish 'our silent colloquy'. The Khevenhüller was sold in 1983. As to his Guarnerius, Yehudi describes it as 'a fellow mercifully absolving the playing of his [Yehudi's] gaffes'. The Guarnerius has an earthly voice, Yehudi says, although it carries on its body the initials, the stigmata, IHS. Jesus hominum salvator.

8

The Man

'DAILY LIFE in Gstaad,' Yehudi's only daughter Zamira told me, 'always began with yoga. Which I loathe. My father, in his underwear, standing on his head, and all of us expected to do the same. Then there would be breakfast, and then he'd disappear, to practise, or dictate letters, or telephone, or chair meetings. Later there would be lunch, and then he'd disappear again. We didn't see that much of him, even in Gstaad.'

Yehudi has four children, two by his first wife, Nola – Zamira, born in California in 1939, and Krov, born in Melbourne, Australia in 1940 – and two by his second wife, Diana – Gerard, born in Edinburgh in 1948, and Jeremy, born in San Francisco in 1951. Zamira is a housewife, now happily married to the Director of the Royal Anthropological Institute. Krov is a distinguished documentary film-maker; Gerard also worked in the film industry, then wrote a cracking novel, a thriller, but subsequently has drifted 'wherever there's employment'; Jeremy is a pianist who, having studied in Paris with Nadia Boulanger and in Vienna with Hans Swarowsky, has carved out a minor career as a soloist, albeit under the long shadow of his father.

'Because of Yehudi's divorce from Nola and the subsequent acrimony,' Krov told me, 'everyone now has their own version of what has happened in our family. So all one can do is scrabble around among particular instances and see if a pattern emerges. I know, for example, that for Yehudi I represent a son from a marriage which failed. I also know that because of all the problems associated with having to look after my mother after the divorce, not least her increasing drink problems, I myself was beset by problems. I had no relationship. I was emotionally drained. I remember when I was about eighteen, for example, having graduated from high school in the United States, coming over to England [where Yehudi was then living] in order to go with a friend to a May Ball at Selwyn College, Cambridge. Before I had left, I had written my father a letter saying I'd love to see him, etc. etc. When I got to England, the reply was awaiting me. No, Yehudi said, this was *not* the time; nothing could be gained from our meeting. I just couldn't understand it,' Krov said. 'It was beyond me. It was as if all the circuit breakers shut off in my brain, and I'm sorry to say that I more or less wrote off my father at that point, and just said, oh well, our relationship doesn't exist any more. I had no feeling. I had no feeling.'

Yehudi told me he could not remember the context in which this exchange took place, putting it down eventually to a moment when Nola 'may have made more mischief than usual. What I find is wretched of Krov,' Yehudi added, 'is that for these last years we have spent more time ... listen[ing] to all his fascinating plans and achievements, and this I have done with Diana's full encouragement. Last summer, for instance, his long-suffering wife wrote Diana a note saying: "To dearest Diny, with thanks for all her efforts to keep the family together." That should speak for itself. Krov probably resents not being what he technically is,' Yehudi concluded, 'i.e. my eldest and first son. The fact that he has done nothing to claim that title does not occur to him.'

Gerard, on the other hand, is not the son of a failed marriage, but Yehudi and Diana's elder child. 'Our family is a bit like a chamber orchestra,' he told me with a sad smile. 'Everyone must keep in tune with one another, and not merely with the first violin, or whatever instrument my mother [sic] might be thought to play. So that when the orchestra is playing together, at the right speed and in tune, the resulting sound, or atmosphere, can be very pleasing. The phrase I would use to describe the atmosphere is perhaps a feeling of controlled formality, although I have to say that even so it is still quite acceptable. Most of the time, however, I'm afraid to say there's an awful lot of bad playing, and one really wouldn't want anyone else, any outsiders, to be present.

'As a family unit we were, well, a little peculiar,' Gerard went on. 'Technically, we *were* a family, but dispersed, because of my father's touring, so in that sense it wasn't much of a unit. And even when we were together, there was a coldness I still find it hard to describe. Meals were always accomplished [Gerard's exact word – he repeated it several times during our interview] very rapidly, three courses in twenty minutes, because my father was always so busy. We had to adhere to a definite standard of neatness, to the point where I always felt sorry for the last piece of ham. The food was, of course, wholesome – I was raised almost entirely without sweets or sugar, soft drinks or white flour – but I would hardly describe meal-times as joyous occasions.

'I know that I became very depressed and very lonely; and I realize now that I grew up without any close friends, and this later became a pattern in my life. One finds that one doesn't know how to develop friendships,' Gerard said. 'One is easily put off by the slightest transgression from what one believes to be one's *ideal* of friendship, which is of course totally unreal because the ideal one has learned comes from books. Yes, I was incredibly lonely. But my father didn't seem to think anything of it at all.

'I once ran away, for instance,' Gerard went on. 'I only got as far as the corner shop in the village, which must have been all of five hundred yards. But as far as I remember my father never asked me *why* I had even felt that way. On the other hand, I suppose one could argue that Jeremy and I, unlike my half-brother and half-sister, as we are *not* products of a broken marriage, had every advantage in life. Thus it was only right and proper that certain obstacles should be deliberately put in our way, to ensure that our progress through life was less smooth. Otherwise, we might by now have become monsters of success. The world can only stand a certain number of successful people, perhaps, and maybe we were not destined to be among that number.'

'I don't know really what he's trying to say,' Yehudi told me of Gerard's outburst. 'He and his mother were incredibly close until Jeremy came along. He never forgave his mother, who from then on had to put up with his difficult, negative behaviour. As for "making no friends",' Yehudi added, 'Gerard had every opportunity, going to excellent school after excellent school in different countries . . . so the fault can only lie in him.'

'People cannot provide what they are unable to provide,' Gerard told me ruefully, 'and it is useless to try and reshape things as if our circumstances could have been any different. In the end, people do not choose their children. So parents must learn to be flexible, very flexible. They must have the time, or *find* the time, to allow new and possibly shocking ideas which are dreamed up, created, by the children, to develop, to make space. In our family, however, that did not seem to be possible.

'Anything that was important to me, I tended to keep to myself,' Gerard added, 'to keep in my own little compartment so that there was no danger of it being damaged. It was the only way I knew how to survive. I can understand how we might have disappointed our parents. After all, what parent does *not* have ambitions for his or her child? To shine, or to be happy. The trouble is that it's always the *same* child; it cannot be exchanged for another, even if it looks as if the child is going to be a disappointment.'

When Gerard was in his mid-thirties, he wrote a novel called *Elmer*, a cops-and-robbers yarn set mostly in Gstaad, the South of France and Paris. It has a certain demi-monde chic: a touch of lesbianism; a hired killer who knocks off (inter alia) noisy motorbikers who disturb the Swiss countryside; a bit of gun-running to Libya. A harmless enough tale, neither too amoral nor too violent nor too sexually explicit to offend most readers of contemporary pulp. Upon publication, it was reasonably well received, not least because it is exceedingly well written. Stylish, tense, economical and witty. Not great literature, by any stretch of the imagination. On the other hand, nothing to be ashamed of. But, as a result of the novel's publication, the already strained relationship between Yehudi and his second son disintegrated entirely. The book was forbidden in the house, and the subject never mentioned. When I asked Yehudi about the book, he smiled wanly and said he couldn't remember. It was all so long ago, he said, although at the time he had written to Gerard expressing his 'revulsion and rejection'. Diana just said the book was horrid.

As we have seen, nothing had prepared Yehudi for the birth of his first child, Zamira. The minutiae of the occasion, the lengths he went to secure 'a Rolls-Royce of a perambulator' flown specially from London, are all vividly recalled and tell a familiar story of proud fatherhood. Careful to the last, Yehudi noted with particular pride that this 'stately vehicle had space enough for Krov, once he was born', although he also remembers that Zamira was 'unfortunately launched' because her nanny insisted on feeding the child Karo syrup!

'Yehudi has always been able to give us the feeling that we've had much more of him than we have actually had,' Zamira told me. 'In fact, we've probably only ever been together as a family for one or two weeks each summer, which is why Gstaad has become so invaluable. We would always *try* to spend Christmas together, and Easter of course. And when we met, they were always such good times that it sustained one throughout the rest of the year. We missed our father, obviously. But then, you can't have everything. If one is privileged enough to have such a father, one must learn to share him. I know that sounds like clap-trap, but it *is* what has been instilled into me, and now I do believe it. When I was a child and still at boarding school, for instance, quite often I had no idea which country he was in! I'm sure my father gave me as much as he *knew* how to give; as much, that is, as he had time left over to give.'

It should not be forgotten, perhaps, that the twelve-year-old

Zamira had opted to leave her own mother, Nola, and move in with Yehudi and her stepmother Diana because (as she told Diana) she 'wanted to be a child before it was too late'. 'She [Zamira] had had to [bear] her mother's total adoration of a brother [Krov],' Yehudi told me, 'only eleven months younger than herself, who usurped all the affection and attention her mother lavished on him. As a result, she became more and more lonely' (Zamira denies this), 'to say nothing of the nightmarish behaviour into which her mother and her friends descended, and of which the poor neglected child was a constant witness.'

I am sure that amid this mayhem Yehudi did his best, that he tried to play the role of attentive and loving father, and that his love for Diana and hers for him and *all* the children, sustained both of them and enabled them to provide what they could for their family. Even Krov, perhaps the most cynical of the children (and, at the same time, the most objective), remembers with affection the many picnics at Alma, California. 'We used to go to the chicken coop together, my father and I,' he told me, 'and he would insist that we eat the freshly laid eggs. Everyone else was horrified, but he loved them. And chocolate-covered ants. He was always coming home with chocolate-covered ants. To this day I can eat almost anything.' Krov was a 'delicate little boy', added Yehudi, although 'always ready to admit his mistakes ... never harbouring ill feelings against anyone else or against himself'.

There is also no question that Yehudi has professed himself inordinately proud of his four children: Zamira, fluent in four languages, musical, a 'brave, self-reliant little girl', 'drawn to the artistic'. Krov, a volunteer with the Special Forces in the American Army, distinguished in 'various hair-raising exploits parachuting from forty thousand feet', 'exploring the floor of the ocean', 'physically fearless', gripped by 'a moral obligation to the natural world', with films on the white whale and the Barrier Reef. 'While Krov was in the Army,' Yehudi remembered, 'the United States government spent thousands of dollars on Krov's preparation for life, and I can assure the government that the money was not spent in vain.' Gerard, 'exclusive' (he and Jeremy were both educated in part at Eton), with 'a high sense of style'; as 'solid and unchallengeable an American citizen as they come … he and I are now closer than ever before'. And Jeremy, 'universally liked' … 'I now have the keenest pleasure,' Yehudi told me, 'in making music with him. He and I seem to feel identically.' Jeremy was the only one of the four children who refused to be interviewed directly for the film. There was too much he might say, he told me, which he knew he would regret.

'I want to tell you of a strange incident which happened to me over twenty years ago,' Krov told me one day. 'By some accident, the invitation I had sent to my grandmother, Marutha, asking her to come to my wedding, was never received. I was most upset, and wrote immediately not only to apologize but to assure her that there had been nothing wilful about my behaviour. Back came the reply saying that it really didn't make any difference. She didn't believe that seeing me or my wife would in any way enhance her own life, and that upon reflection it was silly if we tried to communicate with her again! No best wishes. No enquiries as to the well-being of our marriage. Nothing. Finale. Some years later she did send me a wedding present – a can of dates from California. And I know that if I called her now and said I was going to be in California and I would like to see her, she would say don't bother.

'On one level, of course, such behaviour is very shocking. But on another hand,' Krov added, 'one has to remember Yehudi's own childhood, not to mention Marutha's treatment of Yaltah. Because Marutha thought that the birth of Yaltah threatened to distract her from her cherished task, namely to nurture Yehudi, Marutha simply shut Yaltah out'. What Krov did not tell me was that, according to Yehudi, Marutha's response to his wedding invitation was at least in part a reaction to an earlier letter Gerard had written to her, which spitefully referred to the wayward behaviour of the others. But, as Krov says, it would appear that Menuhins have *always* treated one another in this way.

'At first,' Gerard told me, 'I loved to visit my grandparents. Moshe, for instance, had very interesting ideas about the future of the Palestinians – Palestine was, after all, in some ways his home. Intellectually, Moshe – my father always called him Aba, being the Hebrew for father – Moshe was rather like a suppressed volcano. But as Marutha wasn't always a very sympathetic audience for his ideas, he was often forced to ask over one or two friends for supper so that he could burst out with his political ideas in comparative safety. They also both liked to cook; I recall a frozen soufflé of brick-like consistency made entirely of spinach!

'Anyway, sometimes I desperately wanted to get into the conversation with him,' Gerard said, 'but would usually be cut off in mid-sentence by my grandmother with an interesting remark such as "Would you like some more to eat?" There are so many potential obstructions to growing up and evolving as a useful human being that I did think her attitude a little unfair.' Gerard told me that he began to wonder exactly what obstacles his father had had placed in his way. After all, he said, the most important thing you can give a child is constant love and support and loyalty; above all, perhaps, a feeling of security. And as they came to believe that Marutha had ultimately failed to provide such security for Yehudi, other than in terms of pure dependency, so it was little wonder that they all failed to find it from him, and this has left them all with a terrible burden of loneliness.

Nonetheless, dinner with the Menuhins, *en famille*, can be a most amusing affair. I recall a dinner in Gstaad, prepared by Zamira, with only children and grandchildren present, except Diana and myself. Yehudi was at his most solicitous, insisting on serving all the courses himself, and behaving like a mixture of Father Christmas and Big Daddy. 'Never let Yehudi *near* a kitchen,' Diana told me over the dinner table. 'He's like Ali Baba. Ice cream (which he adores, in spite of all its horrid substances) must be made from at least seventy-five ingredients. There must be chocolate! There must be coffee!

There must be cognac, groundnuts, and even a little bit of garlic. Of course it will taste divine, but it will also take us two days to get the kitchen clean again.' 'Diana always says that Yehudi is absolutely helpless,' Gerard interjects. 'But of course he's not. If you ever go on tour with him, you'll notice that he's absolutely on the ball. He knows who's going where, what's happening here, when the cars are coming, and so on. He will also make sure he has all the right things to eat in his hotel room. And if the layout of the hotel room isn't quite suitable, he'll change it.'

This ability to shape events to his particular and constantly varying needs has always been an essential characteristic of Yehudi's life, right from the time when 'his parents looked after him totally'. 'To this day,' Diana reminded me, 'he likes nothing better than to lie back and have everything done for him. Floating along on his golden barge, with his hand trailing in the water. Sometimes I think he never really left the chrysalis. That somehow he became the butterfly out of the chrysalis and fluttered away, while keeping the chrysalis tied to his tail. Thus he could always creep back into it should he feel the need, to keep away from the rest of us, as it were, even if we are his family.'

Krov – diffident, articulate, almost apologetic for his father's apparent inadequacies as a father – seeks to explain this capacity to 'keep away from the rest of us' with an odd philosophical solipsism. 'Everyone lives on different planes,' he told me. 'You can live on the plane of your family; or you can live on the plane of the community. Each plane is like a concentric circle. Very few people can operate within two of these concentric circles at the same time; for most people, the different concentric circles are antagonistic to one another, if not downright destructive. If you are going to operate successfully as a captain of industry, for instance, and devote yourself to General Motors, you're not going to be operating on that inner circle of family as well you might. But there's also another plane which is cosmic. And if you're operating on a *cosmic* circle, as Yehudi is, it's impossible to operate on either of the inner circles.

And Yehudi has found it increasingly difficult to operate either as a captain of the violin plane, as it were, or as a family man, because the concentric circle onto which he has propelled himself, or *been* propelled, the cosmic plane, has removed him from this possibility.' As he has become a world institution, in other words, the chances of his family (or his violin-playing) surviving untouched have diminished.

I repeat that I would not wish to give the impression that Yehudi has not consistently attempted to be the devoted father. His auto-biography, and many of his other writings, are strewn with loving references to his family and his children, and to his perceived failure to pay as much attention to them as he feels he should have done. 'As a father,' he wrote, 'I probably spent less time with my children than any man not sentenced to life imprisonment . . . I was curiously detached from my children when they were little, and have made close contact with them only as they grew up,' which, as most psychologists would agree, is too late.

Jeremy, the youngest son, is a strange product of this neglect; strange not simply because alone among the children he has opted to be a musician (in spite of his father's active discouragement), but because at first meeting he seems to be the most balanced. He appears happily married, secure in his chosen career, and not obviously at odds with his father or his mother.

I first met him in 1970 when he was nineteen and at the threshold of his concert life. 'I was dominated until I was thirteen not by my mother (my father was never there), but by my nurse,' he told me. 'I was then sucked into a world of privileged education and thereafter into the cloistered world of the professional musician.' Friendship *outside* this magic circle was a serious problem. 'I feel I must have some initial contact,' he told me then, 'which maybe comes from a common love of music, before I can be at ease.' I noticed (and wrote in the *New York Times*) that, as he explained this, he was shifting about nervously on his chair, particularly when I asked him what *kinds* of people he liked. After a long pause, he replied: 'Those who care about music.' And if they don't, I asked? Another long pause. 'I find it . . . difficult,' he said.

I remember feeling that here was a young man trapped in a situation beyond his control or understanding, and I was not surprised to discover recently that Jeremy has spent much of the last few years in and out of various psychotherapies and that he and his wife have parted. 'Once,' he told me, 'classical music was a whole life-style. It affected the way you behaved, your circle of friends, your conversation, your position in society, even the kind of clothes you wore. That is the way it was when Yehudi was brought up. Now, it's just a job. A profession like any other. A forty-hour week with a weekly paycheque. You even need a certificate to belong. You're dressed up in that absurd waiter's suit and wheeled on and off like cultural fodder. It's almost like prostitution' – not, I suspect, a statement with which Yehudi would have much sympathy.

'Originally, I never had any inclination to follow my father,' Jeremy continued. 'At home, everyone called me Fish-Fingers, because I was so clumsy. I think my father reckoned that if I took up the violin, I would drop it. At least the piano is slightly more difficult to drop.' Yehudi duly 'introduced' his son to New York audiences with the American Symphony Orchestra at Philharmonic Hall in New York, in December 1970. They performed the Beethoven C Minor Concerto, 'the only one I knew well enough to play in public,' Jeremy told me. In a French television film made some years later, father and son are seen rehearsing (and disagreeing about) the same concerto. The conflict is painful, not just because there are differences of interpretation, although those are sharp enough. More, that the son appears to have no faith in his father's conducting abilities and is not afraid, or ashamed, to show his disapproval for the benefit of the orchestra. Yehudi, for his part, sails blithely along unaware that behind his back his son is shaking his head and tut-tutting at his father's inability to 'get the music right'. Two souls in disharmony. When I told Diana that Jeremy had refused to be interviewed for my television film, she said:

'Thank God. He would only have come out with all that psycho-twaddle.'

'I find it difficult to say that I love everybody,' Yehudi told me, 'including my own family. But the people in whom I have *faith* have never let me down. I suppose I *would* be disillusioned if my mother ever let me down, but I know that's an impossibility. It could not happen. I was not even disillusioned with Nola, since I accepted that the break-up of my first marriage was as much my fault as hers. And I know I could never be disillusioned with Diana. One often reads in Arabian stories about the passions of first love, of permanent and absolute devotion to a first love, even of dying for love. And when I think of our life together, Diana and I, it has that same element of fairy story.' (Diana was not, of course, Yehudi's first love.) 'A friend of mine, Pierre Bertaud, complained to me that in my autobiography I had written about Diana mostly as an object of absolute devotion,' Yehudi went on. 'As a sophisticated Frenchman, you see, he simply could not understand that one man *could* feel such an absolute about any other person. But I told him that this was possible for me because I had actually experienced it with my own father and mother.'

The truth, as we have seen, was otherwise. As Yaltah told me: 'Mother *never* felt.' It must be admitted again that Yaltah has particular cause to feel resentful about her treatment by Marutha; it is possible too that Yaltah has exaggerated the extent of her ill-treatment. Yehudi certainly thinks so. 'Yaltah had a difficult childhood and adolescence,' Yehudi told me, 'in the sense that she was always compared disadvantageously with her two more serious [sic!] siblings.' Diana can also be occasionally less than charitable about Yaltah's nonstop complaining (a degree of self-pity does run in all members of the family), especially (she says) as Yehudi has constantly had to 'shore up' Yaltah's elder son financially, 'to this day'. But all the evidence suggests that Marutha and Moshe had a tempestuous relationship, made tolerable by their common cause, if not by the idealized world of absolutes in which Yehudi wishes

to believe. Nola's departure was clearly traumatic and disillusion-
ing for all involved. And however sincere Yehudi's apologetic
awareness of the danger to his children that this break-up entailed,
the hard fact remains that each of his children has been hamstrung
in much the same way as Yehudi was. Yaltah told me: 'It was
almost Biblical. The sins of the father, although in our case the
mother, visited upon the children, and upon the children's children. The same tragedy, over and over again.'

As Krov says: 'From about the age of fourteen, I've hardly ever
seen my father. At the beginning this was obviously because of the
divorce, and I felt it was my duty to stay and look after my mother
whom, after a while, my father refused to see. I remember one
time – Diana was already on the scene, but Yehudi and she had not
yet married – my mother was in London and telephoned my father
begging to see him.' Magidoff takes up the story. Nadia Boulanger
was staying with Yehudi at the time, and she said later that Yehudi
had asked her what to do. She refused to get involved in a family
quarrel, she replied. Eventually the answer came back from Yehudi;
no, he absolutely would not see Nola.

'Yehudi could be incredibly ruthless at times,' Krov added. 'A
little while later, for instance, my sister Zamira "decided" to go and
live with Yehudi and Diana. My mother's drinking was, admittedly,
getting out of hand, but even so . . . it was a shattering moment for
my mother to lose her only daughter. It was almost the last straw,
but Yehudi did nothing to discourage Zamira, although he knew –
or he must have known – how it would affect Nola.' Diana admits
that she, at least, realized the emotional consequences for Nola, and
only took Zamira in 'very reluctantly'. The main reason, she now
says, was that Zamira had clearly got scant attention at home. Her
clothes were filthy; her hair was matted; her diet appalling. When
Zamira was aboard, Diana became a devoted mother: 'kindness
and love personified,' Zamira told me.

'Diana began to isolate Yehudi more and more from his previous
marriage,' Krov went on, 'to protect his playing, she always main-

tained. Contact became virtually impossible.' ('Blatantly untrue,' Yehudi says.) 'Until, when I was about twenty-two,' Krov said, 'and serving in the American forces in Germany, Yehudi finally relented and we arranged to meet. At first, it was like talking to a complete stranger. But his natural goodness, his humanity, his childlike qualities, won me over completely. It was all very emotional; twenty years of my life just telescoped into ten minutes.' There were tears in Krov's eyes as he told me this, as there were later when he recalled an attempted reconciliation with his grandmother, Marutha. Certainly, it is hard to believe Yehudi's accusation that Krov has been forever attempting to 'whitewash his mother [Nola], trying to exculpate her ... [ignoring] every bit of evidence of her deplorable behaviour'.

Nor did I sense when talking to Krov any attempt to 'blame' Diana, as Yehudi maintains; quite the contrary. 'I accept of course that he, Yehudi, is very special,' Krov told me. 'One really cannot apply the normal criteria to him that a child would normally expect of a parent. One cannot, for example, reproach him for not being "a good father", because in our circumstances one must realize that this was not on the cards. Because Yehudi *is* this very special person, "family" is not what his life was all about. Little wonder that I've become a nomad. There's no place on earth I can say that I feel more comfortable in than any other place. I am, as it were, without roots.' Diana quite properly reminded me that, nomad or not, Krov has frequently taken advantage of Yehudi's generosity, absent father or not. Krov has often stayed in Yehudi's chalet in Gstaad when Yehudi was not there, and occasionally been the recipient of 'great dollops of Yehudi's cash' when he has needed it.

In a lecture delivered to the Arts Educational Trust in November 1970 at the Golden Lane Theatre in London, entitled 'The Teaching of the Young', Yehudi told a revealing anecdote. Concentration, he argued, is natural in a child. The playing of games and the learning process are as one with a child, and provided the child is given what he or she wants, the child is full of gratitude. 'Have you ever seen the concentration on a child's face as he sits looking at a spider weaving his web?' Yehudi admitted that he could imagine himself spending hours looking at a spider weaving his web, although sadly he had never done so. But 'I *have* seen a spider catch his prey,' he added triumphantly.

One would have thought that Yehudi is far too intelligent not to grasp the implications of what he was admitting – that he was still a child; that as a child he still found the learning process and the playing of games 'as one'; and that what had given him pleasure was the spider catching (and presumably devouring) its prey. It is probably too fanciful to see in this story a mirror of his own childhood, although it is striking that this is precisely the same image that Yaltah used when describing Nola's sanitization by Marutha during their first Atlantic crossing to New York after Yehudi's marriage. Yehudi compounds our problem, moreover, by immediately (in his lecture) going on to describe the normal childhood progression 'from tactile feel to sound, then to sight, and finally to concepts that are purely cerebral'. 'My feeling is,' he continued, 'that when this order is reversed in the child's education, i.e. for instance when the intellectual abstractions occur too soon ... a problematic situation arises, requiring the regeneration of atrophied faculties.' It now seems clear that this is what probably happened in Yehudi's own childhood, although, as we have seen, he has consistently refused to accept this. In a recent BBC interview with one of England's favourite agony aunts, Claire Rayner, he talked yet again about his 'golden childhood' wherein 'no cloud sullied the sky, no tempest disturbed the calm'. It would appear that the truth still hurts too much.

In his Arts Educational Trust lecture, however, he doggedly pursued the truth, although he made it more comfortable for himself (or at least more acceptable) by placing the argument firmly in the third person, or the person of a child not readily identifiable as the author. 'Teaching cannot be separated from society,' he said. (Yehudi, by his own admission, had only one day's public education;

otherwise, he was waiting in that car, watching the world pass by, realizing that most normal activity was 'preposterous'.) 'The terrible results we see today are often the results of the loss of those early years,' he told his audience. (Yaltah: 'Every child goes through a period of great need, of feeling someone should be there. If not a mother, then a teacher or a friend or a relative. In our case, no one was ever there.') 'The little child,' Yehudi continued, 'raised by ... his older brothers and sisters in one room, has more of an environment than the lonely child raised in comfort.' (Gerard: 'Yes, I was extremely lonely ... if one grows up without having close friends, it becomes a pattern later in life.' Gerard and Jeremy both attended Eton – 'for Jeremy it only lasted for a year, thank God.') 'Music,' Yehudi concluded the lecture, 'is the bridge between imagination and reality.' Everything we know about Yehudi suggests that in his case, when reality struck, whether in the shape of Nola or the horror of Belsen, it untuned the music. Music, and what Yehudi hoped were its healing powers, took him to Belsen. And Belsen taught him that, when faced with such a reality, music was inadequate.

When faced with his own family, or when faced with the reality of the family from which he comes, Yehudi has again been forced to accept that his music has proved inadequate. Yehudi would deny this, of course. 'I have had the good fortune,' he says, 'to love music at first hand, from my mother's lullaby to ... my father's Hassidic songs.' Music has not only been his life, his profession and his most important love, but it has also been his spiritual comfort and his glimpse of a world beyond strife, beyond unreason. But the world, as he has reluctantly come to understand it, *is* full of strife, *is* full of unreason. In such a cosmos, music has its rightful place, although Yehudi would admit that music can too easily become 'a ready escape from reality'. 'Music is a wonderful master and mentor,' he told me. 'But I can now see that it should never become an isolated, private Muse ... A musician must constantly renew and retravel the paths of a full experience of living.' And part of that full experience, one would have thought, was family life.

Maybe his own upbringing at the hands of Moshe and Marutha has blighted his comprehension of what constitutes good family life; or maybe (as he often says) his prolonged absences on the concert circuit have prevented him from fulfilling all his acknowledged duties as a father. But even when he has played being father, all the values have somehow got muddled. Gerard's sixth birthday, for instance, was celebrated on board a trans-Atlantic liner. When the birthday cake arrived, it was (according to Diana) a 'severe disappointment'. Yehudi had decided that the demands of good, healthy food outweighed the joy of a good, sticky birthday cake. 'What appeared,' says Diana, 'looked like a flat platter of fish and stewed fruit, held together by a great dollop of wet rope.' Not surprisingly, Gerard burst into tears.

'Marutha has always been an enigma to me,' Yaltah admitted. 'I suppose I never really understood her, and she never understood me. So it's mutual. I'm the contrary to what she would have liked me to be, and she's the contrary of what I would have liked her to be. I would have liked to get to know her better, once the distance was safe, but she didn't want that, so I haven't seen her for years. She is of course a brilliant actress, like Yehudi. But *un*like Yehudi, she lacks a stage. She even lacks a theatre.

'Never forget that she came out of a Middle Eastern childhood,' Yaltah went on, 'a person not knowing the New World except as a harem [sic], as a place for persons seeking opportunity. Her internal images must be very rich; there's always a beautiful Oriental rug over her bed, for example, and I've always believed that this must represent all that is most vivid from her childhood. But psychologically she has dwelled in isolation all her life. A terrible, unfeeling coldness. Now she lives behind closed gates, literally and figuratively. A recluse. Someone who, having gone along with and to some extent encouraged the publicity surrounding Yehudi's early career, refused later to speak in public at all. In private, she has never spoken to us, her children, about her innermost thoughts. I know they've made studies of children who've been raised like that, without real love. Children in institutions get taken care of, I know, but they are not really talked to. I am sure we were loved. But we were not really talked to. So we had our dreams. Later, as you know, Yehudi became deeply interested in yoga and meditation, an admission (for me) that he needed more air and space to breathe in. As children, however, our dream world was wonderful, and, as I've said, in times of trouble, that's the world one goes into, this inner world, because the outer world is collapsing.'

Yehudi, on the other hand, would deny that his 'outer world' has ever collapsed. Like many great men whose preoccupations tend to be cosmic, he prides himself on his practical abilities and his efforts to control that 'outer world'. He could drive a car when he was thirteen, he says, although when he moved to Switzerland he failed the Swiss driving test. He can still pick a lock with one of Diana's curler grips; 'He can get his way in, and out, of *anything*,' Diana told me. 'And he's a master of the telephone.' Wherever he travels by plane throughout the world, he dials Diana immediately he has arrived in the airport terminal. Indeed, Yehudi has a phenomenal memory for telephone numbers, and likes to get much of the business of the day done by calling people from eight o'clock in the morning.

He also likes to cook, though the kitchen is reduced to a post-holocaust shambles as a result. He even likes to wait at table, and no amount of persuasion will prevent him handing round the dishes and serving the food. Illness is something he prefers to avoid, quite simply because it disrupts the schedule. 'Yehudi *never* complains,' Diana told me. 'He always maintains he isn't unwell until he falls flat on his face. Never having gone to school, he never had all those childhood diseases like chickenpox, which is after all one of the few good reasons for going to school, to get childhood diseases. He did once get measles, I remember, when I was about three months gone with my first child. In Cuba. I nursed him through it, and everyone said the child would be born blind, deaf and dumb. Luckily, as you know, Gerard was fine.'

But all the children have had less than straightforward lives. 'At least they have not succumbed to drugs, to alcoholism, to scandal or to any of those troubles that might bring headlines as in the case of other "notorious" fathers,' Yehudi told me. When she was twenty-one, Zamira had married the Chinese pianist Fou Ts'ong. Yehudi admired the long cultural and social tradition from which Fou Ts'ong came, and one of Yehudi's most treasured possessions is a letter written by Fou's father (who was an eminent French scholar) declaring his joy that two of the oldest civilizations in the world, the Chinese and the Jewish, should thus be joined together. The letter had been written in the traditional Chinese manner, with a brush.

But the marriage was a failure, and ended after a few years. Hephzibah had married Nola's brother, to some extent chosen for her by Marutha, in spite of being deeply in love with someone else at the time. Her marriage had also collapsed. Later she found some happiness with an Austrian social worker employed in Australia, Richard Hauser, although that relationship also ended in disillusion.

Yaltah, meanwhile, during one of the many absences of Moshe and Yehudi, had been urged by Marutha to elope to Gretna Green, Scotland, with one Keith Pulvermacher. Yaltah had gone down to the lobby of the Grosvenor Hotel in London to meet Pulvermacher with a coat and handbag given her by Marutha as a parting gift. But unable to leave Hephzibah, with whom she had shared her childhood as the family toured the world, at the last minute Yaltah had turned round and gone back upstairs. This had so angered her mother that she ignored Yaltah totally for weeks.

William Stix had by now written from St Louis proposing marriage to Hephzibah. Marutha had dictated Hephzibah's reply, in which Hephzibah wrote *she* could not accept, but would Yaltah do! Broken down by constant harsh treatment, Yaltah agreed and a marriage was hastily arranged to coincide with the family's return home via New York. Thus the day after the boat arrived in New

York Yaltah was married to William Stix in the offices of Judge Pecora. Her mother dressed her in black for her wedding.

Not surprisingly, Yaltah's marriage lasted only six months and, at its end, Marutha wanted Yaltah to divorce Stix on the grounds the marriage had never been consummated. Yaltah refused. She now remembers little about her marriage, but back at the family home, alone with Marutha, Yaltah soon developed asthma and hypothyroidism, two complaints from which she still suffers. A second marriage in 1940 to Benjamin Rolfe, a lawyer then drafted into the army, by whom Yaltah later had two sons, Lionel and Robert, also ended miserably. Throughout this eighteen-year marriage (not mentioned by Yehudi in his autobiography), Yaltah combined a career as a pianist with that of being a wife and mother. But Rolfe's jealousy of Yaltah's music was a factor in the breakdown of their marriage. When Rolfe began to lock Yaltah out of their home (literally), she knew she would have to leave, and did so in 1958. In 1959 Yaltah met the pianist Joel Ryce in London, where she was scheduled to play a concert with Yehudi and Hephzibah. Joel and Yaltah married in 1960. Due to a hand injury, Ryce retrained as a Jungian analyst and now works in private practice in London. 'Silly', was Yehudi's description of Joel's contribution to the film.

Hephzibah had two sons – Kronrod and Marston – by Lindsay Nicholas, and a daughter, Clara, by Richard Hauser. Marriage at least gave her some perspective on the influence of Marutha. In a letter to Yaltah in 1946 she wrote:

'Life is too short to waste on incompatibilities or on the efforts we have made in the past to appear extraordinary and deserving. That is what Australians call 'bunkum' and we are not at all extraordinary, not any of us, not even Yehudi – except in our queerness and maladjustments. Yehudi has a great heart and a magnificent intellect – lots of great men have – but he hasn't a drop of 'horse sense' and that is why his [own] marriage might have gone on the rocks ... I blame Yehudi foremost – not Yehudi as such but his ignorance for allowing a high-spirited, strong and beautiful young wife to want 'love and brightness'. He could not keep her at that cost, and as to her own fallacies, if he hadn't been his mother's son he could have had the strength and courage to lead Nola into a better life, instead of taking orders from Marutha and then relaying them secondhand to his wife.'

Later, in the same letter Hephzibah added: 'You are right in saying that [Marutha] never knew happiness and that is why she lived through us. Proxy was as near as she came to romance, and because it was unattainable she longed for it all the more, through our letters, our love experiments. She hungers for it so much that, like starved humans, she would feed on it at the cost of destroying it. It is pathetic and bloodcurdling and [Moshe's] role in their matriarchal scheme is even more repulsive than anything else. He is a martyr, and, being a Jew, he has a depth of capacity for enduring pain which wrings one's heart. He has been so repressed, so beaten, so thwarted, so humiliated that perhaps he has no one opinion of his own at all. [Marutha's] cruel handling of us all – and of you in particular, Yaltah, because you had the most elusive spirit and are also the least well defended, is the spiritual counterpart of cannibalism. Perhaps I have said enough. But there is one more thing to be yet said in all justice; because of what [Marutha] did give, and because of what she has suffered, we owe her an allegiance not to put any obstacle in her way in case she ever determined to be human.'

The full story of the relationship between Moshe and Marutha will probably never be known, although the suicide of Moshe's favourite sister must have damaged his belief in the sanctity of human relationships, and Marutha herself was also (as we have seen) the child of a broken marriage. 'How can a family, how can *people*, go through everything and especially marriage and bearing children,' Yaltah asked me, 'without being in touch with their own true feelings? No wonder all of us have failed so often in our attempts to reach out and touch other people.' As Hephzibah wrote,

'[Our upbringing had] made awful fools of us when we faced our first life situations.'

The paradox is, of course, that Yehudi – even if he were to admit the burden that 'family' has imposed upon him – would argue that 'family' is the most important factor in his life. He never stops telling the world of its importance, both for himself (his 'golden childhood') and for society ('it is to life that I owe my allegiance'). But no family is perfect, and why should he, with all his other commitments, be expected to have produced the perfect family?

'A musician must be a trusted object offering his fellow men solace,' he says. In 1974 he inaugurated the Musicians' International Mutual Aid Fund, as a result of which various musicians promised to join him 'in concerts in the capitals of the world and play for any cause I wished'. An admirable vocation, and not necessarily inimical to the preservation of strong family ties. But I think it not too fanciful to suggest that Yehudi's fear, his awareness that somehow his own family life is not as he would have wished, and certainly not as he wishes the rest of us to believe, has propelled him increasingly into this concern for a *world* family. Individual failures cannot be laid at his door; on a global scale, he can accept that he has 'accomplished very little'. He can admit that his own life and aspirations present 'a sorry balance sheet', but in the global balance sheet of an International Mutual Aid Fund, he does not have to include members of his own family. 'He was delighted to have children,' Gerard told me, 'and he spared us as much time as he could. We always had a good family Christmas. My mother and father were a fine team. But often children do not evolve in the way parents wish, although I think we have probably emerged fairly unscathed in the circumstances. I want to keep a sense of humour about this.

'When I was thirteen or fourteen,' Gerard went on, 'I desperately wanted to run away from school. One or two of my fellow pupils actually did. Others tried other escapes; one committed suicide. Even at the time I remember feeling profoundly cut off, especially when I was allowed back home for two months or so of the year. It was a home of sorts, I suppose, with its familiar belongings and my books. But where else could I have gone? If I had had any close friends, any friends at all, who might have given me some support, I might have been a bit more adventurous. But I wasn't.

'Years later, when I had written my novel,' he told me, 'I never dared show it to my father, although I know he's read it. It was far better that I didn't take the risk of hearing him criticize it and then being disappointed.' Gerard has worked diligently in the film industry in France and the United States, and bridles at his parents' suggestion that he has never earned his living. And even if he was less than forthcoming to me about Yehudi's enormous generosity to him, both in terms of cash and in providing a place for him to live during the summer months, his complaints must have some element of truth. 'As children,' he told me, 'we were a bit like tomatoes. (As I said, we need to keep a sense of humour about this.) Tomatoes need to be watered, every day. It's a nuisance, I know, but unless they are watered, they die. Tomatoes can be very rewarding. They grow red and you eat them. Now my mother is very disciplined, and would have been perfectly capable of watering the tomatoes. It's an investment. A bit like Woody Allen's roses; at least they're not always borrowing money. But with children, I've always felt that my parents were asking: "Are they going to repay the investment?"'

Yehudi has often described his children in terms of a reincarnation of his own parents. Gerard and Jeremy; Moshe and Marutha. Gerard (Moshe), 'exclusive, conservative, with a fiery temper'; Jeremy (Marutha), 'investigative, self-analytical, mercurial'. And it is inevitable that in trying to make an assessment of Yehudi as a man, one is drawn back again and again to the formidable, if diminutive, figure of Marutha. As I write, she is old and frail, but still capable of dominating any conversation. She still addresses Yehudi as 'child', and scolds him publicly for his misdemeanours. 'I'm sure you have plenty of secret thoughts,' she said to him in front of me. 'Strictly your own, of course. And of course love affairs.' To me she said, wagging her finger, 'He was always in love with *somebody*. Oh, he was a mischievous little boy,' she went on. 'I don't say wicked, because there wasn't an ounce of wickedness in him. But he certainly took a premeditated pleasure in shocking people. We grown-ups were always being made fun of, but Yehudi was always diplomatic, always careful not to put himself in the wrong light.'

It was such an improbable meeting. Yehudi, almost seventy-five, white-haired, slightly bent, much smaller than one might expect, seated at a table opposite his ninety-six-year-old mother, dressed in black, with a large, floppy black hat tied by a ribbon under her chin, a white shirt with a ruff collar, a wig, dark glasses to hide (and protect) those dancing eyes; a slightly squeaky, high-pitched voice, but long, elegant fingers. She cannot have been more than five feet tall, but she perched on a chair in the sitting room of her house in Los Gatos, the same house where she lived with Moshe for over fifty years, sipping champagne, holding court like the Oriental queen that she is.

'Just think,' she said, looking at me and my film camera. 'Hollywood come to Kimberley Avenue. Now, *you* know, Yehudi, that I am a very private person, and here you are expecting me to perform like an *actress*!' 'I propose a toast,' said Yehudi, trying to prevent Marutha from taking complete control. 'A toast to all the women in my life; Diana, of course, but especially, my mother!' Marutha smiled, and then added: 'Yes. That's true. Without me, you wouldn't be here. So, gentlemen, this is my last chance to put the people straight. It's my duty, to tell the truth, due to my venerable age. I'm an old woman now, and don't you forget it. Gentlemen, you must always try to speak out, and tell the people what you stand for; what is worthwhile in life, and what is *not* worthwhile in life.'

In a well-researched book published in 1978, Yaltah's elder son, Lionel Rolfe, proved beyond any reasonable doubt that Marutha's claim to be Tartar was a fantasy. Her parents, Nathum Sher and

Sarah Liba, were entirely Jewish. From the beginning, it seems, Yehudi's mother has created a world wherein fact and fiction are irredeemably confused, the consequences of which have burdened almost beyond endurance her children and her children's children.

9

The Artist

THE LIVES of most performing artists settle very early into an annual pattern which changes little for the rest of their career. Such is its blessing and its curse. The regularity of such a career, which some quickly discern as crushing monotony, is broken only by an act of will or physical disability. The venues may change; one year the artist might go round the world west to east, next year east to west; but the concertos remain the same and so do the hotels. The challenges – emotional or intellectual – decrease, and a terrible weariness sets in like gangrene. Those who survive (both as artists and as human beings) a lifetime on the road are few. Many abandon their careers, some get married, a few go mad. Yehudi is among the very few who have survived.

And yet, since his thirty-fifth birthday when he set off on that memorable journey to India, his life – and his schedule – have proceeded at first sight year in year out with numbing regularity. A new festival here, a new symposium there; more lately the switch from performing to conducting when he could no longer consistently play the violin to his own high satisfaction. But the most cursory glance at his diary reveals a sameness which even a bank clerk would find a little dull.

There is a tacit recognition of this in Yehudi's autobiography. Written when he was almost sixty, two-thirds of the book concerns his life pre-1952; and of the remaining one-third, over half is preoccupied with general observations as to the nature of the universe and man's place in it. In other words, less than a sixth of the whole tells the story of most of his middle years. This cannot be because there is nothing to tell; the Bath and Windsor Festivals, the Gstaad Festival, his involvement with the International Music Council, are all post-1952. It would appear instead to be an acceptance that little in his adult life could match the newness, the excitement of his astonishing youth. This is understandable enough when one remembers all that befell Yehudi in the first thirty years of his life. When most people's careers are beginning to catch fire, Yehudi's – in some senses – was over. But the admission also seems to me to reflect Yehudi's increasingly anxious search for a role, a purpose, a usefulness other than that of a peripatetic violinist. Time is running out, even if – as he happily says – thus far his life has been 'a wonderful adventure'.

In her own memoir of their life together, *Fiddler's Moll*, Diana entitled the two most revealing chapters 'Log Book (Part 1)' and 'Log Book (Part 2)'. Their tone is breathless, relentless and scary. The first log book covers the period February 1953 until December 1957, almost five years in twenty-two pages. The second overlaps, beginning in June 1957 and ending in October 1958 with a visit to Pablo Casals in Prades. In 'Log Book (Part 1)', the Menuhins visit Mexico, Paris (four times), California (twice), London (many times), Athens, Munich, New York (several times), Budapest, Lago Maggiore, Capetown, Switzerland and Washington. Among others, they meet Merle Oberon, Rubinstein, Toscanini, Krishna Menon, King Paul and Queen Frederica of the Hellenes, Wilhelm Kempff, Oistrakh, Khatchaturian, Karsavina, Nadia Boulanger, Benjamin Britten, the Queen Mother (several times), the Queen of the Belgians, Enesco, and Mathilde Kschessinskaya, the last mistress of the Tsar from whose balcony 'Lenin had chosen to announce the Revolution of 1917!' And all this apart from speaking to or having dinner with more or less every ambassador you can think of. No wonder that Yehudi had so little time to practise.

No doubt if one studied the schedule of a prime minister or a member of the British Royal Family, one would find their diaries equally full. But that is precisely the point; even given the international life-style of many great contemporary opera singers or conductors, very few could match Yehudi's 'log book'. It's almost as if he *were* royalty or at least a head of state. The fact that he is a violinist is almost irrelevant. And this is the life he has been leading, year in year out, for almost seventy years.

Paradoxically, Yehudi has protected himself against the stress of constant touring by preserving as much continuity in his travels as he can. Thus, when he descends upon New York or Berlin for the umpteenth time, it is as close to a homecoming as he can arrange – the same hotels, the same concert halls, even the same agents: Menuhin is proud of the fact that in most countries of the world, the same agents (or their sons, or their grandsons!) still represent him as they (or their forebears) did when he began touring in the 1920s. In Germany, for instance, the family Adler; in Spain and Latin America, the family of Ernesto de Quesada who only relinquished Yehudi when de Quesada died, aged ninety-five; in America by Columbia Concerts, whose founders Laurence Evans and Jack Salter had originally signed Yehudi in 1924; in France, three generations of the family Dandelots have passed Yehudi along, father to son.

In the days when he travelled principally as a violinist, his violin cases – containing the tools of his trade – were packed by his father with meticulous precision. But the 'tools' were far more than a violin and bow. His cases were full of knickknacks to remind him of home; indeed, he often seemed to carry around so much junk that the violin case itself came to represent home since it carried all the accoutrements necessary for a nomad's tent. In the case which protects his 1742 Lord Wilton Guarnerius, for example, one finds a piece of rock from Yehudi's cottage on Mykonos; endless pictures of Diana – eating watermelons, swimming, cooking, generally clowning about; a bottle of cleaning fluid, Benzin, to clean the violin's fingerboard; numerous chamois leathers; a Kashmiri shawl, embroidered on both sides, a souvenir of his Indian transmogrification and also a reminder of his mother's Eastern ancestry; scissors (several pairs) for the nails; a little French bag full of spare handkerchiefs; combs (many); an Art Nouveau cross given to Yehudi by a nun whom he had known for fifty years as a symbol of her devotion to him; a picture of Buddha – 'all religions are here represented,' he told me with a smile; a curious-looking washing-line peg which, he explained, is used to thread new violin strings; a baton 'given me by Pandit Nehru'; a doeskin to protect the violin; various old love letters; a gold medal, the significance of which Yehudi has forgotten; a box full of miniature decorations to be worn in the lapel of his evening suit – the British Order of Merit, the French Commander of the Légion d'Honneur, the Dutch Order of Oranje Nassau and 'this rather curious little one. Italian, I think. You can tell it's Italian because it's more gaudy than the rest. I always carry this box, so I can never be caught out for my evening wear no matter what country I turn up in'; another silver box – this one full of snuff, a memento from his mother-in-law; a length of plastic pipe 'which I put under the fingerboard in humid weather to prevent it sagging'; a wooden chock which, if he is giving a recital containing a Bach solo sonata, for instance, he will wedge into the sustaining pedal of a grand piano thus enabling it to act as a resonator for the violin's harmonics; spare pairs of reading glasses; a heavy violin mute which allows him to practise in his hotel room 'without annoying the neighbours, and without me having to hear my own sound too loudly'; a peacock feather; pictures of his father and mother; pictures of his two sons by Diana; a clock-like device to check on the humidity in the violin case; a 'hand of Fatima' which 'used to be encrusted with all kinds of spangles' – 'The hand of Fatima is supposed to bring good luck,' he told me. 'We got it in Tunis the year Jeremy was born [1951], and it's been in my violin case ever since'; various seashells and a secret compartment containing numerous small coins – Germany 1929, George V sovereign, Canadian five dollars, Italy 1948.

'When I was a child, my father gave me a double violin case,' Yehudi said, 'lined with antelope and covered in pigskin, with room for four bows. I remember it was enormously heavy; it *still* is enormously heavy, so how I managed as a child I do not know. At one point I had two Stradivarii and two Guarnerii, but then I thought that was a bit too much for a mere violinist, so I traded one of them in to buy my London house. But I still have my original violin, a Grancino, seven-eighths normal size. My mother and I found it in 42nd Street in New York when I was seven; one of my father's Hebrew teachers bought it for me at a cost of seven or eight hundred dollars, and it was on this that I gave all my earliest concerts until Mr Henry Goldman gave me my first full-size violin, the Prince Khevenhüller, in 1928.'

The Khevenhüller family had sold its Stradivarius violin in 1825 to Josef Böhm, also of Vienna, who was the teacher of Joachim (for whom Brahms wrote his Violin Concerto). Böhm in his turn had sold it to Popov, Professor of Music in St Petersburg, from whom a Jewish American dealer, Emil Herrman, had bought it after the revolution in 1917. And Herrman it was who had sold it (at Yehudi's request) to Henry Goldman. Thus the violin had only four owners before Yehudi. Yehudi was amused to discover later that a Stradivarius owned by Fritz Kreisler, the other great 'American' violinist (he was actually Austrian), was made within three months of the Khevenhüller. Indeed, several great violinists owned Stradivarii of the same period; that of Adolf Busch, Yehudi's teacher in Basel, had been made in 1732; that of Ysaÿe, another of Yehudi's teachers, in the same year.

Yehudi's second authentic Stradivarius was not acquired until 1951, when he bought the instrument known as the Soil, made in 1714 and named after the nineteenth-century Belgian collector of violins M. Soil. Once again, the instrument was acquired through Emil Herrman. Generally thought to be among the greatest of all Stradivarii, principally because of its power and precision, it was this instrument that Yehudi eventually sold 'in exchange for my house'. Curiously, at one time Yehudi also owned a third 'Stradivarius'. After the gift of the Khevenhüller, Yehudi became so worried about the wear and tear on the violin resulting from his nomadic life-style that he commissioned an exact copy of his Khevenhüller from the French violin-maker, Emile Français, on which he could practise. So perfect was the result that it sometimes amused Yehudi to use the copy in concert so as to confuse the critics who, of course, could not tell the difference.

It was none of the Stradivarii, however, which eventually became Yehudi's soul-mate. It was the Guarneri del Gesù of 1742 which Yehudi says he bought (also from Emil Herrman!) in 1939. He still has it, describing it as his 'holy of holies'. It has 'a voice at once heavenly and earthy, somehow untutored, somehow magical', he told me.

I asked him whether, sixty-two years on, performing in public with *any* of his violins still gave him the same thrill; or had the years of playing dulled the excitement? Without hesitation, he replied: 'Oh, I still feel vulnerable. As an artist, a violinist has to stand upon the stage, his two hands doing totally different things at different angles. I also feel absolutely wretched if the concert has not gone well. There's no great mystery about this. A violinist *knows* when he has not played well, or he's not in good form, or he hasn't worked enough, or he hasn't had a chance to learn the piece thoroughly. I know some musicians who will walk out of a concert they are not satisfied with. But I could never do that, not just because I would not want to let down the management or the public, but because I want to collect the fee! That's as good a reason as any to keep going!

'Of course there are occasions when I've been in a bad mood,' Yehudi told me, 'or worried about something, and consequently have not been able to give of my best. But I believe I know more about the violin now than I ever did before, and therefore I have greater pleasure in playing now than I ever had before. I feel I play with less wear and tear, less tension. Admittedly I can't do everything now that I used to be able to do. But as artists, violinists are a curious breed. Against all odds, they can often express on the violin their innermost feelings in a way that is not open to many other instrumentalists. They can convey themselves directly to the public and hopefully carry the public with them, even when, technically, the playing is less than perfect. I remember that was true of Enesco at the end of his life, for instance. He was still capable of quite stunning performances, even though his back was almost bent double and his fingers crippled with arthritis. It's not always those who have flawless techniques who give the most moving performances.'

Yehudi often refers to his adult life as an artist not simply in terms of a lost innocence (many creative artists do that), but in terms of 'robbery' and 'theft'. Maturity 'robbed him of intuition', he writes, although the 'theft' has been compensated for by an extra measure of insight. This ignores the fact that what distinguished his earlier recordings is precisely this insight, and that too many of his later recordings (and performances) are distinguished not by insight but by faulty technique. Arpeggios and scales, practised relentlessly, day after day, hour after hour, might well have cured this faulty technique. But for Yehudi, such a remedy would only have been 'hit-and-miss', since it would have 'robbed him' of his primary role, that of being an interpreter; or, as he rather quaintly puts it, 'more than a simple transmitter'. Being an interpreter involves 'conveying a message', although 'an understanding of the composer's style' and the physical mastery needed to translate that style into actual notes are clearly important. But again, Yehudi is disarmingly honest when he defends interpretation (as opposed to merely having a perfect technique) as 'a very slight unevenness, originating in personal feeling. I would feel *robbed* if I could not rely on my personal feelings.' Personal feelings, as we all know, can be notoriously unreliable, and I'm sure that Yehudi's personal feelings are more volatile than most. So, in admitting that this reliance on personal feelings can sometimes result in 'a very slight unevenness', Yehudi is almost acknowledging his own shortcomings as a violinist.

Technical mastery is, for Yehudi, a series of 'automatic responses to impulse'. This explanation could be used of course to cover up a multitude of sins, except that few performing artists take as many risks in performance as Yehudi does. Almost every time he steps on the stage, or chooses to 'prop up a cathedral', or play in a lunchtime concert at some aircraft factory during the war, he challenges himself (and his audience) with a high-wire act of derring-do. Will he or won't he make it? Nothing is ever safe about a Menuhin recital. I suspect this has always been so, not least because of his fascination with Bach. No composer has written violin music which demands such dazzling technique; no composer has written music which is so cruelly exposing, so merciless to the performer. Anything *less* than technical mastery will be immediately audible to the listener. Yet the great Bach Chaconne in D Minor, the summit of all violin writing, was in Yehudi's first ever recital in the Carnegie Hall in 1927 when he was eleven.

Yehudi had learned the Bach Chaconne with Enesco while on holiday at his teacher's country estate at Sinaia in Romania. Enesco wrote later: 'Whoever penetrates the tragedy and the faith [of this Chaconne] . . . has understood the human soul. It is incomprehensible but, at the age of eleven, Yehudi seems to have understood it. Genius is a miracle about which one can say: I know not the why and wherefores of it, but it could not have been otherwise. It would be futile to question Yehudi about his, because he will not know how to speak of it. All he can do is perform the miracle again from time to time, and that is more than is given to most mortals.'

It is tempting to dismiss this eulogy as the melodramatic ramblings of a mad – and highly excitable – Romanian composer/violinist for his latest pupil, especially when one learns from Enesco's letters that the lessons apparently took place during a violent thunderstorm! But one knows that Yehudi's other influential teachers – Persinger and Adolf Busch – felt much the same way when describing their pupil's knowledge of Bach. And in his prime, no concert or recital by Yehudi was without a Bach sonata or partita. The recordings he made in 1975/6 of all three partitas (the Chaconne is from Partita

No. 2) and all three sonatas, remain some of the most important in the catalogue, not because of their technical wizardry (again there is a liberal dose of wrong notes), but because of their profound grasp of the material. If Yehudi's performances are not always *academically* acceptable – and there are endless musicological disputes as to exactly what Bach intended in terms of tempi and ornaments – they are heart-stopping in their intensity and emotional bravura. In Enesco's somewhat colourful description, 'It is as if Yehudi has lifted the enormous weight of human fears and hopes and, unbruised, carried it through that thunderstorm.' It is probably sufficient – and more accurate – to say that Yehudi's 1975/6 recordings are the standard by which all others are measured, now and for the conceivable future.

Again it is the depth of understanding which marks out these recordings as special; and although one knows from his pre-war recordings (he first recorded the Chaconne in May 1934) that this comprehension was already there when he was young, there is little doubt that his experiences of the war must have enriched his understanding. There was, for instance, an extraordinary concert in the Aleutian Islands (between Siberia and Alaska) where the temperature was thirty degrees below freezing. According to his accompanist, Adolph Baller, even those keys on the upright piano which worked were out of tune. Yehudi had no choice but to play unaccompanied; not hits such as 'Pistol-Packing Momma', which was then popular with the troops (and which he could play), but Bach sonatas and partitas, most of which must have been a complete mystery to his audience. Baller remembered one recital which consisted of the E Major Partita, the G Minor Sonata and, of course, the Chaconne.

Indeed, when one looks down the list of Yehudi's early recordings, one is constantly flabbergasted by the risks such a young artist was taking. Alas, many of these early recordings are deleted or lost, and many Yehudi does not even admit to. But from his first recording on 12 March 1928, when he was eleven, until the occasion

when he re-recorded the Elgar Concerto with the New Phil-
harmonia Orchestra under Sir Adrian Boult at Christmas 1965, the
endless variety of his repertoire is what must, in part, have kept him
fresh as an artist. During that period – thirty-seven years – he made
approximately three hundred and sixty recordings, that is almost
one a month. Admittedly all of the early recordings were 78 rpm,
lasting no more than five minutes per side. But it is a towering
achievement. In the first year alone, apart from his debut with
Achron's 'La Romanesca', there were works by Bloch, Handel,
Fiocco and Ries (all with Persinger at the piano). The following
year included Bach, Beethoven, Mozart, Corelli and Paganini. The
Bruch Concerto followed in 1931, Mozart and Bach concertos the
following year (his recording of the Mozart concerto K271a, made
on 4 June 1932 when he was just sixteen and conducted by Enesco,
has never been surpassed in technical excellence, musical insight and
richness of tone); and finally the Elgar Concerto on 15 July 1932.
Recordings of Schumann, more Paganini, Nováček, Wieniawski,
Schubert, Rimsky-Korsakov, de Falla, Enesco, Brahms, Dvořák,
Debussy, Sarasate, Szymonowski, more Beethoven, Ravel, Gran-
ados, Rossini, Mendelssohn, Pizzetti and Bartók followed with
bewildering speed – and all these before he was twenty-one. Most
were made with Enesco conducting; for years Yehudi insisted that
Enesco supervise *all* his recordings, such was the young man's trust
in his mentor.

Apart from anything else, the money those recordings earned
must have been phenomenal. Yehudi has always been somewhat
coy about discussing the money-making machine he was in his
youth, and has continued to be so ever since. Partly this is because
he would naturally reckon such matters to be private (and, what's
more, irrelevant to his art), and partly I suspect because he doesn't
know. Moshe handled such matters when Yehudi was a child, and
subsequently there have always been agents, lawyers and secretaries.
The money he earned as a boy undoubtedly gave him – and his
parents – freedom, or what he thought of as freedom, and the

money he earned was breathtaking. In 1928, for instance, Moshe boasted that he had turned down over two hundred thousand dollars' worth of offers (maybe five million dollars at today's values), and the same again for 1929. Even the Soviet government apologized (in 1931) that it was not able to guarantee more than six thousand dollars *per concert* (eighty to ninety thousand dollars today). Hollywood offered Yehudi a two-million-dollar contract in 1938 for the rights to his life story, which was rejected out of hand. 'Between Yehudi's musical art and Hollywood,' Moshe was reported as saying, 'there is an abyss that cannot be bridged. The pure ... art of Mozart and Bach, and Hollywood's synthetic made-to-order art are ... irreconcilable worlds which no fakir, no money and no whitewashing can bring together.' But two million dollars! Maybe twenty million dollars in today's values! Hollywood, being Hollywood, couldn't believe that the Menuhins could say no. Emissaries were sent from Los Angeles to New York, where Yehudi was playing. 'They actually thought I was crazy, or else I wanted more money,' Yehudi told a reporter. Moshe reacted more grumpily: 'We wouldn't sell our soul for *all* the money in Hollywood,' he said. 'Artistic integrity means more to us than riches.' The irony is that today's Yehudi would probably have accepted the offer and loved the experience.

To be fair, Moshe and Marutha did their best to protect their son from this deluge of riches and adulation. And when one thinks of the rock stars in the late sixties who did not have the benefit of such protection, one's admiration for Moshe and Marutha increases. Janis Joplin, Jimi Hendrix, Mama Cass, Jim Morrison, Keith Moon, John Bonham – all drowned in a sea of drugs and alcohol, victims of excess, unable to cope with riches and adulation.

And Yehudi *was* their equivalent in the late twenties and early thirties. He was more admired than any politician; he was better *known* than any politician. There were no popular music entertainers who could rival his capacity to draw the crowd – over six thousand at the Oakland Auditorium when he was seven years old! He was a film star without ever having appeared in a movie, and yet he was only a violinist. An artist. No wonder Hollywood wanted him. It was, for instance, not possible to 'walk in the park, as other children did', as Yaltah complained, but not for the reasons Yaltah told me. Women would throw themselves at Moshe 'to kiss the father of so phenomenal a boy'. Vast crowds would gather outside the Menuhin house on Steiner Street in San Francisco to catch a glimpse of the boy genius. Some would even crash through the front door demanding that their children be allowed to play with Hephzibah and Yaltah. Newspapers kept up a constant demand for interviews, and Moshe became adept at what would now be described as 'sound-bites'. With unwitting irony, Moshe told the *San Francisco Chronicle*: 'The responsibility of bringing up a child [like Yehudi] is very often more than a parent can perfectly fulfil.'

Paradoxically again, the more Yehudi became invisible – in the most time-honoured pop-star tradition – the more lavish the epithets that were heaped upon him. 'America's Pride', read one headline; the 'Goliath of the Violin', read another (Yehudi was nine at the time); the 'Caruso of the Violin'; the 'Orpheus of the Violin'; the 'Einstein of the Violin'; best of all was 'Uncle Sam's King David of the Violin'. Endless syndicated articles appeared under such titles as 'Strange As It May Seem . . .'; or 'This Curious World'. 'The Boy Wonder' was a headline which greeted his debut recital at the Scottish Rite Hall in San Francisco. Soon this was clearly not enough. Before long he became 'The Miracle Boy'; then 'Menuhin the Great'; then the 'Violinist of the Century'; finally 'one of the world's intellectual prodigies'. And he was only twelve years old!

There was no escape. He was known for his 'wit'; others would call it rudeness. A man barged into his dressing room backstage one night after a concert, for instance, announcing: 'I am Mischa Elman's father.' (Elman was one of the great violinists of the day.) Yehudi did not react. Whereupon the man repeated: 'I am Mischa Elman's father!' Again Yehudi did not react. Frustrated, the man shouted: '*I* am Mischa Elman's father,' to which Yehudi politely replied: 'And what else have you done for him, sir?' Not very funny, but immediately repeated and reprinted in a hundred newspapers across the United States.

Fan letters arrived by the sackload. A girl from Tennessee wrote on a postcard: 'Dear Friend: I saw in the papers where you want to get married.' (*Had* he said that? He could not remember. He was, after all, only fourteen.) 'When you receive this card,' the girl went on, 'you can send me your picture and I can send you mine. I am sixteen years old and a brunette.' In fact, it was Marutha who was already marrying off her children. In the *Woman's Home Companion*, she wrote: 'We are very anxious for Yehudi, Hephzibah and Yaltah to marry young.' (Marutha, after all, had married when she was nineteen.) 'It may be a little difficult for them to find their proper mates,' she said, 'because [my children] are not sophisticated in the way in which many young people are sophisticated today. Yehudi says if only he could find someone a little like Hephzibah, and Hephzibah adores her brother and compares all other boys to him.' When asked what her own ambitions were for the children, Marutha replied with startling directness: 'A little colony of Menuhins on the Los Gatos hills.'

We have seen the consequences of this intolerable pressure, although it is easy enough to forgive Moshe and Marutha for what might otherwise be seen as merely blunders in bringing up Yehudi. Even Krov admits 'they had no data, no guidebook, to help them shape and mould the artist'. And I doubt if Yehudi was just the roly-poly angel-face that he is sometimes portrayed as being. Enesco noted that 'Yehudi is like a vineyard on top of Vesuvius. There is the vineyard, all peaceful and still, thriving in the warm sun and the blue skies. But under that lovely vineyard is a volcano.' Yehudi's temper – and his capacity to sulk – was legendary. At a family picnic in Yosemite, for instance, Yehudi once left the breakfast table without asking permission. 'Yehudi,' shouted Marutha, 'you must ask to be excused before you leave.' But Yehudi would not do so, and so was ordered to resume his seat. This he did, but remained there for hours, scowling. A true artistic temperament, you might say. On another occasion he was beaten vigorously with his father's belt when he refused to apologize for a misdemeanour. This stubbornness, reinforced by a steely determination, has always been a characteristic of Yehudi the man and Yehudi the artist. When I first discussed making a film biography of Yehudi, a friend told me: 'Beware the iron fist in the velvet glove.'

Part of this stubbornness he got from his mother who never forgot, and often never forgave. She would 'brood', according to Yaltah, 'spreading a gloom through the entire household'. 'Everyone moved about in shrouds for days and days,' she remembered. But part of Yehudi's behaviour obviously stemmed from his being spoiled. He told his first biographer, Robert Magidoff, that until he was eighteen he 'never crossed a street unescorted. It was a strange, awkward and exhilarating experience, as was my first contact with the telephone. Previously,' Yehudi said, 'all the telephoning had been done for me, so that the phone had become a symbol of intrusion by the outside world (and remained so for many years).' Like most children, Yehudi wore pyjamas. But underneath the pyjamas, he was forced to wear heavy woollen underwear. He told a friend: 'My mother makes me wear it all through the spring, even if I perspire and am terribly uncomfortable.' 'Then why not wear regular underwear?' asked the friend. 'My mother thinks it is better this way,' Yehudi replied, adding: 'I shall be making my own decisions after I am twenty-one.'

We now know that there were very few decisions he was allowed to make before that time. Marutha's constant invocation of her own mother was interpreted by the children as the force (and tradition) of law, from the necessity of mustard plasters to the desirability of certain drinks such as fermented mare's milk – much better for you, said Marutha, than cow's milk – and black bread cider known as kvass. The only exception to this dietary control was ice cream. In almost every contemporary newspaper article about 'the boy wonder', there is a reference to Yehudi's addiction to ice cream or ice-cream soda. Even concert promoters, such as Walter Damrosch in New York, knew that Yehudi's reward for a good concert was a dish of ice cream. Once, a large prima donna from the Metropolitan Opera House said to Yehudi: 'How much do *you* get for filling a concert hall?' 'An ice cream,' he replied. 'And by the way, strawberry is my favourite.'

And because the ice cream was invariably a gift from his parents, it came to have a meaning way beyond its immediate taste. 'It was a symbol of my parents' joint approval,' he recalled, and 'gladdened me as no ovation ever could. If my performance brought happiness [to them], this gave my ice cream a flavour no manufacturer in the world could imitate.'

This simple pleasure contrasts sadly with what one knows about the other 'pleasures' of his childhood, or those of his sisters. Yaltah recalls that when she was about ten or eleven, for example, she had wanted to imitate the fashionable hairstyles of the time (1931). Marutha absolutely forbade Yaltah to cut off any of her long, blonde curls. Naturally, Yaltah rebelled and snipped off one side of her hair. Marutha was furious and shaved her entire head, claiming that her own mother (again) had always said that a bald scalp was good for you once in a while, since it cleansed the mind and spirit, not to mention the scalp. Yaltah was, of course, mortified, and even when Yehudi and Hephzibah offered to shave their own heads out of sympathy and solidarity, Yaltah's tears could not be assuaged. Yehudi has a different recollection of this event. 'Yaltah always loved her hair; she would sit in front of the mirror and comb her golden tresses. She *still* can't be separated from them, even though they now look ridiculous on her rather wizened face. But, anyway, we came back one day to find she'd been experimenting with hair tongs and had made great patches on her scalp. Whereupon my mother said, "Well, there's only one way to cure that, and that is to cut all your hair off." And having done that, she said to my sister and me, "It would be nice if you two would do the same, to keep her company."'

'A child who is the product of a fully harmonious union,' Moshe told a friend, 'has a greater "genius capacity" than a child of brilliant heredity who is blocked by the inharmonious union of his parents. Show me a perfect union, and I will show you a perfect child. Ability or genius is but the absence of friction in the human organism, so (in our case) there is nothing for Yehudi to overcome in the mastery of the violin.' Even if this were true, can this really be the source of Yehudi's artistry? One knows that the marriage between Moshe and Marutha was rather less than a perfect union. One knows that they left scars on all their children. One knows that each child was ill-prepared for the world, with unfortunate consequences. And yet one also knows that, before he was twenty-one, Yehudi had made dozens of recordings of music whose depths he had glimpsed and was able to communicate.

Perhaps there is a clue in what Yehudi describes as the strengths he admires in other musicians, particularly those conductors under whom (and with whom) he has performed. Bruno Walter, for whom Yehudi first played in 1929 in Berlin (the 'Mayflower' concert) was 'gentle'; Toscanini 'friendly and easy'; Karl Muck, 'a man of high principle and character, upright in every way'; Adrian Boult, 'a gift for concentrating on the essentials, always striving for perfection of ensemble'; Monteux, 'benevolent and good-hearted, yet always able to project his overall vision of the music'; Klemperer, 'telepathic, a man for whom the intention was somehow loosened from outward means of expression'; Beecham, 'exhilarating to make music with because he always saw with a fresh eye'; Furtwängler, 'a human being who evoked music'.

All of these epithets are, of course, also descriptions of Yehudi the artist. Bruno Walter said to Yehudi that he would give anything to hear the great works again for the first time; in other words 'to recapture that first moment, that first hour, in which one meets a loved one'. For Yehudi, the works of Beethoven or Bach or Bartók are also described in terms of 'friendship', a relationship which is renewed and enriched upon every meeting. Friends cannot be ignored or they disappear. Neither can they be treated with abject deference. They need constant attention, like tomatoes.

This personal approach to his artistry was further exemplified when Yehudi was once asked to compare his playing with that of Heifetz. 'Heifetz is an acrobat,' Yehudi said. 'He is like a tightrope-walker who must give a similar performance each time, no matter what his life's experience may be, otherwise he will fall off the wire. His performance must be absolutely reliable technically, therefore, correcting his balance between very narrow limits, an example of supreme discipline. I, on the other hand, am a clown, or a mime artist. It is essential that my emotions affect my actions. I must *live* every moment, and so I believe that these moments become deeper, more feeling, more subtle with each passing year. The acrobat and the clown are quite different, even if they are both part of the same circus.'

'As an artist, I believe it is imperative to make this connection between my playing and my life,' Yehudi told me. Some years ago, he elaborated on this theory to Robin Daniels, a music critic who was also a social worker in South London. 'An individual needs to be integrated into a collective system, and yet at the same time feel free and independent,' Yehudi said. 'He can't feel free if he's held back by an arbitrary kind of restraint. Just so with the violinist, and in particular the violinist's left hand; for each finger to be able to respond freely, all the joints need to react in coordination. Each finger *wants* to be able to move independently, but to achieve this there must be no resistance in the other joints. They must act in support and cooperation. Thus it seems to me that the principles governing my knowledge of the fingerboard and my experience of life are very similar – a balance between freedom, and the impediments to freedom, between the analysis of problems together with the logical resolution of those problems, and restraints such as prejudice, selfishness and greed.'

Yehudi has since extended this principle into an entire rationalization of his role as an artist. An artist is a servant, he says, and no artist is justified in believing that what he or she does is of 'excessive importance'. Art is 'inseparable from nature'; thus 'no human-created art is without its counterpart in the animal world. Art begins as self-dialogue, and ends with what we see of ourselves and others, and what they see of themselves and us. As an artist,' Yehudi told me, 'I yearn for a balance between the perfect equilibrium of the womb, and the environment of constant movement in which we exist. Happiness, and by that I mean our/my fulfilment as an artist, is not a feeling or condition I aim for in the future, but a conception of balance that I believe was alive deep within me from my earliest experience of the womb.

'I know, however, that much art is *not* created out of this feeling of happiness; nor is it necessarily created by men and women of high moral purpose,' Yehudi added. 'Those enslaved by alcohol or drug addiction are equally capable of creating great art. But I am an interpreter rather than a creator, although obviously the two are not mutually exclusive. And I could never perform were I thus enslaved. Of course, I know that jazz and even Indian music is often created under such conditions; but, for all my involvement in those cultures, I come from a different tradition. I must be aware of my own pulse. I can never be dependent on audience reaction or any extraneous comment, otherwise I would never attain the serenity I seek. I *do* know that, on those occasions when I have attained this serenity, this balance, I can hold a vast audience in a kind of magical suspense. Public performance is, after all, a communal experience, with everyone sharing similar emotions,' Yehudi told me in conclusion. 'The soloist is the mouthpiece of that essential power which comes from the group.'

Fritz Kreisler was once asked (by Robert Magidoff) to analyse what it was that made Yehudi's artistry so unique. (After all, the Elgar Violin Concerto had been dedicated to Kreisler, and first performed by him.) For one great violinist to comment publicly on the strengths and weaknesses of another great violinist might seem a little bizarre, and it says much for Kreisler that he approached the task with his customary sangfroid. After all, both had been child prodigies and both had become legends before their physical maturity. Kreisler knew at first hand the problems (and traumas) with which Yehudi must have been confronted. 'Most of us take the major part of a lifetime to develop the gifts nature has bestowed upon us,' Kreisler said. 'But the miracle of Yehudi consisted in that by the age of twelve or fourteen he had fulfilled a very large part of what nature had given him. [As a result,] I foresaw that he would have great difficulties,' Kreisler added. 'Some of these difficulties, fortunately, proved to be rooted ... within his listeners, who ... expected Yehudi to grow and mature after adolescence at a rate comparable to that of the period preceding it.

'Our age is an age of speed,' Kreisler continued, 'whereas maturity and growth are slow processes. Yehudi has been growing steadily ... against the heaviest odds, such odds as have actually destroyed most prodigies. He has [also] achieved the artist's most difficult goal; he remains himself. The tempo of an artist lies not in the metronome, but in the pulse beating inside him, for great music is *adjustable* to the personality of the artist playing it. Listening to Yehudi, I sense a pure, noble mind, an understanding and, above all, a constant growth.'

'Maturity as an artist is not won easily,' the music critic of the *New York Times* wrote after Yehudi's Carnegie Hall recital in January 1953. 'There has been indication [recently] of a struggle going on within him ... [but] whatever private difficulties he has had with his art, he seems to have conquered them.' Other discerning critics noticed a similar sea-change. The *New York Herald Tribune* wrote: 'No other violinist has such speaking eloquence in the tone alone. [Most of] our young performers are settling for intellectual athleticism. Yet it is his very wholeness that enables Menuhin to speak intelligently from the heart and reach – as he ever has – the heart of audiences.'

We can now have sympathy with this 'struggle going on within him', and have some notion of its destructive effect. We can now understand Diana's first shocked reaction at hearing Yehudi play – 'Something had gone wrong. It was as if the violin had become his enemy' – and we can comprehend her lifelong struggle 'to put Humpty-Dumpty back together again', and indeed admire her success at having done so. Her loving transformation of the violinist into the institution has been remarkable. If both Diana and Yehudi have sought to rewrite history – he about his 'golden childhood', she, for instance, about their first encounter (she remembers his 'golden skin' and that he was 'intolerably healthy'; others, at the time, remember Yehudi as being flabby and pale and permanently tired) – this is understandable. When they requested Yehudi's first biographer, Robert Magidoff, to delete numerous passages from his text of which they did not approve, this is less forgivable, even if they had the contractural right to do so.

What has become abundantly clear, however, is that the crucial change between his early and his later playing is not the failure of technique, but the closer and closer identification of the man and what he is trying to tell us through his playing. A musician's first duty, he told the Incorporated Society of Musicians in 1965, is to society. The 'nature of music combats everything in life which is formless or indiscriminate. Music thus provides standards of thought, insight and effort by which other activities can be judged.'

In fact, Yehudi's first duty has always been instinctively to himself, a paradoxical situation for a man so dedicated to becoming a 'citizen of the world'. Partly this has been a reaction to the suffocating influence of his parents; partly to hide the guilt which has dogged him since he escaped from his parents to marry Nola, and then got found out like a naughty schoolboy. Partly this explains the raw deal some of his four children feel they have had at his hands as a parent, a feeling not entirely justified in view of his generosity to each of them. But chiefly, this has been his strength as a creative artist. 'Every life has a price,' Yaltah reminded me, 'and maybe every human being pays far too great a price for that life. We were taught to believe that. So in Yehudi's case perhaps, and for his great gift, no price has been too great.'

Sir Neville Cardus, the eminent English music critic, wrote in his memoirs, *Full Score*: 'Sooner or later, every masterful technician in the arts comes face to face with the problem the young Menuhin was called upon to tackle. Can he ever become an artist who can re-create? [Some violinists] have contented themselves with the art of glorifying and ennobling the violin. Menuhin is a musical seeker ... To arrive at a state of musical dedication which did not fetter self-exploration, Menuhin was obliged to submit to a psychological change *endangering* [my italics] such superficialities as "exact intonation". A Menuhin performance is endowed, however, with life, nerve and the pulsating, always questioning, intelligence of the man himself.'

As he approached his seventy-fifth year, Yehudi told me that he greatly regretted he had had so little time for reflection. An old friend, Willa Cather, Aunt Willa, the distinguished writer whom Yehudi had first met in New York in 1930, had once given him a valuable piece of advice, he said. Quoting Shakespeare's *The Tempest*, she told him: 'What's past is prologue.' 'The very nature of your work,' she had written to him, 'means "pack your kit".' He has never ceased to do precisely that.

Trying to make an appointment with him in the 1990s often means booking him weeks in advance. He has a secretary, an agent, her secretary, a full-time research assistant, housekeeper, travel agent and, of course, the indefatigable Diana. He's writing a religious column for *The Times* of London, an article for *The Times* of India, and a letter to the *New York Times*. He's planning a tour of Japan with the newly-formed Asian Youth Orchestra, and refusing to perform in China as a result of the massacre in Tiananmen Square. He's flying to San Francisco to visit his ninety-six-year-old mother; he's flying to Berlin to play in a concert for the newly reunited city; he's flying to Warsaw to perform more Mozart symphonies for his new record contract; he's flying to Paris to be made a member of the Académie Française; he's flying to Toronto to receive the Glenn Gould Memorial Medal. He's being filmed for a television documentary to celebrate his seventy-fifth birthday; he's being interviewed in English for yet another radio programme about his childhood; he's being interviewed in French about his ambition to open a Menuhin School of Music in France; he's being interviewed in German about his plans for this year's Gstaad Festival. He's trying to catalogue the thousands of photographs in his collection, because only he knows the exact identity of some of those in the pictures – Elgar, Karajan, Nehru and so forth are obvious; but equally valuable from an historical point of view, if less well known, are Yehudi with Adolph Busch in 1929, with Piatigorsky in 1932, with Bruno Walter in 1934, with Shostakovich in 1945.

Above all, he is still making music. He is still alive as an artist. Conducting has given him an extra lease of life, an extension to an already extended career. He pretends not to read reviews, but various articles in the British newspapers, following a less than successful performance of the Beethoven Concerto in the mid-1980s, stung him deeply. Consequently, as a violinist he prefers not to perform in Britain now, except with his School Orchestra. And while it is true that respect for him has declined among international orchestras, the public's appetite for Yehudi Menuhin remains unquenchable. Whether in Berlin or Vienna, in Moscow or Tokyo, in New York or Warsaw, his concerts are always completely sold out. Only Maria Callas and von Karajan outsell Yehudi in the gramophone catalogue, and both of them are dead.

The last paragraph of his autobiography begins: 'I am looking forward to ...' And his motto throughout the whole book is: 'I have never resigned myself.' As a child, Marutha had taught him that life was an inexorable journey towards the light. And his autobiography is entitled, after all, *Unfinished Journey*.

10

A Death in the Family

'Until Hephzibah died,' Yehudi told me one morning, 'I had never lost any member of my family. We knew she was dying and that her days were numbered. She had been suffering from cancer for years, and we had tried various doctors in various places, all to no effect. The day she died, at the beginning of January 1981, I was in Gstaad, and supposed to be giving a violin lesson. I am sorry to say that I delayed leaving until after I had given that violin lesson, much the same reaction as my mother had had when news reached her in San Francisco of the death of *her* mother. Her mother had died in Jaffa, in Palestine, and nobody had meant more to my mother than her mother. But when the telegram came, all she did was take me out in the Chevrolet to deliver a child's potty to a neighbour because it was no longer of any use to us. In other words, she went on more determinedly than ever, almost as if nothing had happened. In her heart, of course, she must have been very sad, even bitter because my father had prevented her from visiting Palestine to see her mother two or three years before.

'And in Hephzibah's case,' Yehudi said, 'it was the same, I'm sure. But no, perhaps there *was* something else. The truth is that I think it was the circumstances of her life that killed her as much as anything else, and what must have been for her a terrible disillusion. It's horrid to think that this disillusionment grew and grew towards the end of her life, and that this is what, partly, brought her to the end. One hopes that one's journey through life is, inexorably, towards the light, and not towards the darkness. But the end of *her* life was darker by the day.'

Hephzibah – the desired one. Can there ever have been a brother and sister so devoted to one another? Years earlier, for instance, when the Menuhin family had first decamped to Paris, and where Yehudi had first declared his intention of studying with Enesco, the sojourn had not been quite the happy, carefree existence that Yehudi has consistently maintained ever since. Homesick, wracked by guilt with the growing knowledge that it was he who was already the family breadwinner, the eleven-year-old Yehudi had often become dejected and weary. He had suffered regularly from nightmares; once he had awoken to the sound of gunshots, followed by screams. A murder had taken place in the courtyard below, and the following morning there was blood on the cobblestones. Hephzibah had held his hand while he cried. Another night he had dreamed he was being pursued by a monstrous giant; as he cried out for help, it was again the seven-year-old Hephzibah who had comforted him. When his parents had come rushing in to calm the tormented child, Yehudi had felt so embarrassed that he vowed never to call for help again. Nonetheless, Hephzibah had continued to succour him. Later, Yehudi would remark that 'her trust in me ... was so natural that it survived public appearance ... The understanding, trust and ease of relationship ... revealed that we had a Siamese soul.' And now she was dead.

Above all, perhaps, she had been his conscience, for it was she who had first spelled out the confusion of their lives. 'We learned through untold suffering,' she had written to him, 'that the twentieth century was not to be run according to the commandments that had governed our childhood. [We were brought up to believe in] work – holy, absolute work, performed in the spirit of extreme self-giving – and the rest was not important. [But] all our music helped not at all to build a humane life. Before the wreckage of those early dreams, we had to admit that our claim to early success was infinitely smaller off-stage than on-stage. Before the responsibility of our growing children, we had no other standards than those against which we had to measure up ourselves. And these had . . . failed us.'

And it was Hephzibah, with Yaltah, who had constantly reminded Yehudi of the damage the *family* had done to Nola. When the newly-married Yehudi and Nola had returned to New York on board the *Île de France*, for example, after their marriage in the Caxton Hall registry office, Moshe had secured the largest suite on the boat – for the family. Nola had been expected to share this suite with the rest of the family. Thus, she had been told to order her breakfast in French (a language she obviously did not speak) as this was a French boat. She had caught a cold, and although she had at first refused to accept the family cure of a mustard plaster, Marutha had insisted that Nola take scalding hot baths; 'that scorching hot water certainly killed the cold,' Nola said later, 'but at the time I thought I'd go with it.'

Meals, of course, were taken in private, as they always had been, to keep the Menuhin 'children' away from the prying eyes of the public. According to Hephzibah, Nola was asked at the first dinner where she would like her suitcases, as they were full of all the honeymoon clothes. 'Oh,' interrupted Marutha, 'they can stay in the hold.' 'But all my evening clothes are in those cases,' protested Nola. 'Well you won't be wanting any of those on *this* trip,' said Marutha.

Yehudi was told by his father that he should not kiss or caress his bride in public, as this would be unbecoming for a Menuhin. And when Yehudi almost inevitably caught Nola's cold, Nola was publicly rebuked by Marutha, and Yehudi told to take his daily walks upon the boat deck accompanied only by 'members of his family'. In their private moments (and how could there have been many in a shared suite, however presidential?), Yehudi was advised to read Nola the collected works of Pirandello 'so that she could learn Italian'. Nola also had to endure sarcastic remarks about her hand-made lingerie, a wedding present from her father (how were *these* inspected?), and told never to eat double-decker sandwiches (a harmless enough Australian obsession) because it was 'plebeian'.

The shock of such treatment also scalded Yaltah and Hephzibah more surely than any hot bath, and they too never forgot or forgave. And this to someone of whom, as we have seen, Yaltah could still say over fifty years later with tears in her eyes, 'She was our bridge to youth, because she was a real young woman.' Yaltah was then abruptly dispatched to Washington the day after the *Île de France* docked to meet up with William Stix, who was about to take up a government post. Hephzibah remembered waving farewell to Yaltah at Grand Central Station, the little girl clutching her battered school briefcase in which were some of her favourite musical scores, a volume of French poetry and 'a notebook full of her own childhood verse'. She cried and looked pathetic, and she was not yet seventeen.

And Hephzibah? Married a month later in Los Gatos to Nola's brother, thus being obliged to cancel her first concert as a soloist with the New York Philharmonic. As she wrote to the director of the orchestra: 'I will ... go with my husband where he has his own house [in Australia] to cheer his solitude, to play the piano for him, to teach him the Italian language and animate the monotonous plateaux of his immense property with winged vision.' At least Hephzibah kept a spark of independence in her belly. As the SS *Mariposa* left San Francisco Bay for Australia with the newly-weds on board, she grabbed all the heavily-boned corsets Marutha had given her as a wedding present (she later told Yehudi), and hurled them into the ocean.

Yehudi, on the other hand, had hurled nothing into the ocean. Even if all the stories about Nola's later drunkenness and love affairs are true; even if it is the case that Nola spent all Yehudi's money and left him more or less penniless by the time he met Diana, there is no doubt that Nola suffered woefully. Soon after their marriage, she had discovered a list of instructions from Moshe about Yehudi's daily needs: a long walk, eau-de-Cologne for a rub-down during the intervals of concerts, ten dollars in an inside pocket for tipping. Nola had responded in the only way she could, by conceiving Yehudi's child. Zamira – 'for peace', 'the songbird'. The birth inevitably brought Yehudi great joy, but what he has never admitted is that Nola insisted Yehudi be present at the birth, equipped with a surgeon's mask and gown. A common enough experience today, but in 1939 extremely unusual. And the Guarneri del Gesù he acquired at the time – his 'holy of holies' – was not bought by him from Emil Herrman, but given to him by Nola to celebrate the birth of Zamira. He had wanted to buy it, but had decided it was too expensive. After discussion with Moshe, Nola, whose family was not without means, had found the money. By comparison, Hephzibah was already finding life in Australia a strain: 'I have sacrificed everything I have loved up to now,' she wrote. And Yaltah was already divorced, and already planning a second marriage, to Benjamin Rolfe from Los Angeles. The 'Biblical Family Menuhin', as Enesco described them, were plunging head-long towards the unknown.

In fact, most of Yehudi's childhood dealings with women *other* than his sisters or mother were plagued with disaster, and not just the disasters normally associated with adolescence or simply growing up. His great love for Rosalie Leventritt, for instance, had had one horrific moment which haunted Yehudi for years. He had been to lunch with the Leventritts who were, after all, family friends. Afterwards, on an impulse, he took Rosalie to a matinee. Apart from the fact that this involved crossing a street without the aid of his parents, the whole expedition was accomplished without Marutha's permission! Never mind that he was seventeen; never mind that Rosalie was more or less approved of. As a result of the matinee, Marutha demanded that Yehudi promise he would never ever do any such thing again.

Yehudi obeyed, of course, but friends noticed that he soon became sullen and apathetic. Not for the last time, his violin-playing was affected. Then the newspapers became aware. One headline read: 'Yehudi, Violin Dictator, Does Not Answer His Father Back'. Moshe was described as 'an elderly satyr', a 'centaur' ... 'edging about his son'. Even Dr and Mrs Garbat, old friends from New York who had introduced the Menuhins to Yehudi's first patron, the banker Henry Goldman, were eventually so dismayed by Marutha's treatment of Yehudi (and of Hephzibah and Yaltah) that they slowly disentangled themselves from the relationship.

This must have been especially difficult for Mrs Garbat, who, as Rachel Lubarsky, had been a fellow student with Moshe some fifteen years earlier. But, try as she might, she could not abide (or understand) Marutha. She had a daughter about the same age as Hephzibah, called Fifi. Fifi had wanted to give two of her dolls to Hephzibah and Yaltah as presents. Marutha sent the dolls back, with a note from Hephzibah saying: 'My mother says that to play with dolls is a waste of time.' After all, Hephzibah and Yaltah had each other, and both of them had Yehudi. As Hephzibah wrote later: 'I was always in terror of losing that link which represented full happiness and security.' But the Garbats had had enough; enough of Marutha scolding Moshe about giving too many interviews on Yehudi's behalf – 'It was so undignified'; enough of Marutha refusing to allow Yehudi the most innocent and childlike of pleasures. Once, after a long country walk together, the Menuhins had been asked back to dine with the Garbats. A large turkey had been placed on the table, whereupon the ten-year-old Yehudi had exclaimed with delight: 'Oh, what a turkey! Everybody can eat all they want!' Marutha was furious, told Yehudi off for his greed, and sent him from the room.

Like most young adolescents, Yehudi found it difficult to understand why any young woman of his choice did not fall instantly in love with him. Sidney Ehrman, 'Uncle Sidney', was, as we have seen, another of Yehudi's early patrons; indeed, he had provided the money – a 'loan', as Marutha insists to this day – which allowed the Menuhins to make their first trip to Europe, to Ysaÿe and to Enesco. Sidney Ehrman had a beautiful daughter, Esther, to whom Yehudi undoubtedly lost his heart when he had first met her, aged nine. Soon she gave him a Chinese puzzle-ring – four small intertwined rings – which was a copy of one she always wore herself. Yehudi was smitten.

Once, he held her hand all the way to a concert in the Civic Auditorium in San Francisco. In the dressing room, he discovered that his hand still smelled of Esther's perfume and so refused to wash until the perfume had long vanished. Yehudi tried everything to capture Esther's heart. He had heard that she admired Heifetz playing Schubert's 'Ave Maria', so the next time he knew she was going to be in the audience, he included the piece as an encore. On another occasion, he had been frantically searching his pockets for a handkerchief with which to mop his brow after the first movement of a particularly taxing concerto he was performing with the San Francisco Symphony. To his surprise and delight, Esther, who was sitting in the audience next to Marutha, had come forward and offered her handkerchief, to immense roars of approval from the audience. Yehudi had been deeply embarrassed, but refused to return the handkerchief after the concert.

Yehudi carried around the Chinese puzzle-ring in his violin case, wrapped in Esther's handkerchief, for years. Even Sarah Kreindler, who had beaten Yehudi in his first violin 'competition' in November 1921, left a scar. Sarah had played Sarasate's 'Gypsy Airs' which had 'justly merited first place'. Yehudi had played the Beethoven Minuet in G (not 'Remembrance', as he sometimes says). Although at the time the five-year-old Yehudi had shown no visible signs of disappointment at having come second, internally he must have been distraught. Not only did he never play the Beethoven minuet again – at least, not for over thirty years – but, in his autobiography, he mis-remembers what he actually played.

Years later when, as Mrs Lazard, Esther was asked about her childhood romance with Yehudi, she remarked calmly that there had been no romance, merely marriage to the entire family. After all, she implied, Yehudi had had his sisters, and that was enough. Indeed, even those friendships which Marutha allowed, soon discovered the limits of that friendship. The family Fleg, for instance, had been brought into the Menuhin circle in Paris by Enesco, and came therefore with the 'highest possible credentials'. (Fleg *père* had written the libretto for Enesco's opera, *Oedipe*.) The Flegs had two sons, Maurice and Daniel, Daniel being the same age as Yehudi. The two had got along famously, so when Yehudi returned to San Francisco, he asked Daniel to join him on holiday.

The following year, 1937, Daniel Fleg arrived at Los Gatos, somewhat the worse for wear after the trans-Atlantic journey. Daniel kept a diary of those days (published in 1941), and from this unique, outsider's record emerges what is now, for us, a familiar picture. At first Marutha nursed Daniel back to health, with 'angelic patience and implacable will'. She reminded Daniel of 'a little lady Buddha, very delicate and fine'. Soon Rosalie Leventritt came to stay, and her letters home are equally revealing. 'Yehudi's mother is very beautiful,' she wrote, 'with her wonderfully blue eyes and dusty blonde hair . . . she has the loveliness of a kitten.' The fourteen-year-old Yaltah soon fell in love with Daniel, writing him love poetry in French, English and Italian; Yehudi, as we have seen, fell hopelessly in love with Rosalie. They swam together, walked together, played Mozart together, were altogether inseparable, noted Daniel. But, he added, they never kissed.

Marutha was *always* on hand to prevent even an embrace. '[Marutha] always finds a place to sit on that is quite high,' wrote Daniel, 'so that she keeps an eye on everything, to guide, to dominate. She never raises her voice, but everyone does as she wants them to.' Rosalie added, in another letter: 'With Yehudi's mother, you are always aware of the steel claws you cannot see.' 'Madame Menuhin presents an entirely different manifestation of force,' Daniel said. 'I find there is something excessive, almost offensive in the way in which [Yehudi] is hovered over, and is to such a small degree master of his moves and life . . . this respect and admiration for the parents is of a . . . menacing degree.'

When Daniel suggested that the children drive out for a picnic to Carmel, Marutha at first refused. She only relented after Daniel promised Moshe that he, and not Yehudi, would drive the car. Yehudi was, after all, only twenty years old. Yehudi of course disobeyed and drove the car himself as soon as they were out of sight of Los Gatos. Unfortunately, upon their return, with Yehudi still driving, Moshe was waiting on the doorstep. Daniel Fleg fell from favour like a stone in water. Although Yehudi (with Nola and Moshe) saw Daniel again, briefly, in the South of France during the spring of 1939, Daniel's journal suggests that this rebuff at the hands of the family Menuhin was a severe blow.

He had always been frail in health and spirit, and six months later he drowned himself in the Seine. It was also Daniel's brother, Maurice, who had fallen in love with Hephzibah (and she with him), written to declare his love and had his letter intercepted by Marutha, thus allowing Marutha time to arrange Hephzibah's marriage to Lindsay Nicholas.

After Yehudi himself was married, the symbiotic relationship with his sisters continued. 'I would have followed him anywhere,' Hephzibah wrote later. 'To be related to Yehudi means to be part of the endless miracle of life.' The feeling was mutual. Referring specifically to their musical partnership, Yehudi said: 'I do not believe there ever existed a partnership more naturally, instinctively perfect than ours.' Paradoxically, Marutha's disapproval of Hephzibah's concert career heightened the brother–sister relationship. Marutha told Hephzibah: 'A woman's place is in her home. The only immortality to which a woman should aspire is that of a home and children.'

'[Yehudi] often commented adversely on my cold efficiency,' Hephzibah said, 'and asked me if in fact I was as unfeeling as I seemed. I was not, of course, but I *was* very ashamed of expressing my emotions.' Speaking of their concert appearances together, Hephzibah added: 'We were such a team ... all I know is that with such a partner, one simply had nothing to risk.' The critics noticed another element. At the end of a successful concert together, Yehudi and Hephzibah would more or less ignore the shouting and applauding audience except for the most cursory nod. Most of the time they just held hands and smiled at each other. Marutha, on the other hand, told the *San Francisco Chronicle* that she 'always praised Hephzibah far more for a well-balanced, well-executed dinner cooked by her, than for any concert she ever played with her brother'.

'Is Yehudi ever alone?' a reporter once asked Moshe. 'No, never,' came the instant reply. 'We are always with him – to take care of him.' The reporter was amazed; Yehudi was eighteen at the time. 'Where are those hours when a youth dreams in the sun?' the reporter continued in his column. Then, warming to his vision, he added: 'Where hide those moments of delicious loneliness, when a boy sits by himself beside a river?' The answer is that there were none, because Hephzibah was always there. And when she wasn't, Yehudi became listless. Another childhood friend, Lydia Perera, kept a diary during this period, when she too had become fond of Yehudi. One entry reads: 'March 22, 1936. Concert in Town Hall, mobs rushing through the centre aisle, shouting their acclaim. Yehudi looks tired and weak.' Another entry says: 'Yehudi looks tired, indifferent and sad. I had to grit my teeth as I left the Hall, to keep from crying.' Admittedly those entries came at the end of a phenomenal year in Yehudi's career; one hundred and ten concerts in sixty-three cities in thirteen different countries, and this before the age of air travel. But Lydia Perera's friend, Rosalie Leventritt, told Robert Magidoff: 'All we would say, looking at him, was: "Oh no, it cannot be!" and left it at that. We somehow could not get through to him, even when his parents weren't around.'

Hephzibah's first marriage lasted longer than those of her brother or her sister. While it would be an exaggeration to say that she had married Nola's brother on the rebound from being abandoned (as she came to think of it) by her real brother, it is a familiar enough pattern for siblings whose emotional relationship is strong to marry a relative of the partner of their brother/sister in order to preserve what they can of an earlier and more cherished love. In the beginning, after their marriages, events had conspired to keep Hephzibah and her brother apart. She was taken off to a sheep farm in Australia; he continued his peripatetic career. But it is strange that, as soon as Yehudi's marriage with Nola broke down, Hephzibah reappeared on the scene as a musical partner.

It is unclear why the marriage between Hephzibah and Lindsay Nicholas collapsed, but having an absentee wife cannot have helped. Nor could the sight of the drunken Nola (who had returned to Australia for a while) have endeared Hephzibah to Nola's brother, even if he was her husband. Whatever the truth, Hephzibah and Yehudi resumed their joint career soon after the end of the Second World War with a concert at the Metropolitan Opera House in New York. Hephzibah brought her two sons, Kronrod and Marston; Yaltah brought her son by Benjamin Rolfe, Lionel; Diana was by now on the scene. And when Yehudi made his pioneering tour of the new (and hostile) state of Israel in 1950, Hephzibah was again there, complete with armed guard. They visited the kibbutzim together; they played for the President of Israel, Chaim Weizmann, at his private residence; they met General Dayan together. Interestingly, they found Weizmann preoccupied not by the Arabs who surrounded his new state – after all, the Israelis had already endured one war for their survival – but by the possibility that now the Israelis had their own land, they would forget those characteristics which had distinguished them throughout the diaspora: 'the passionate need [of the Jew] to rise above danger and endemic persecution and prove himself; his self-containment and determination to reach the highest possible position in whatever ... profession he uses his brain'. One can imagine the effect that such an injunction from such a man had on the newly reunited brother and sister.

When Yehudi started his festival in Gstaad, almost the first person to play there was Hephzibah. And when he went to Russia, Hephzibah went too, speaking fluent Russian, searching out forgotten

Menuhin cousins, and showing Diana the churches of Moscow. When one reads Diana's diary of this visit, one senses the same conspiratorial atmosphere (us against them) that had pervaded the Menuhin household when Yehudi, Hephzibah and Yaltah were children. The car which had met the Menuhins at the airport, for instance, black enough and cavernous enough to house 'the coffin of an Enemy of the Regime'; the 'splintered parquet of [their] bedroom'; 'the tepid bath-water'; 'the skimpy curtains [in their bedrooms] hanging like shrunken washing from their peeling gold poles'; Hephzibah practising 'on a golden piano covered with cupids and simpering ladies'. It must have seemed to Hephzibah and Yehudi much like their first trip to Paris and Berlin over thirty years earlier. A source of endless giggles and adventure. The joy is that Diana seems to have understood this and, with her natural abrasiveness, become the cheerleader, effortlessly 'bashing' (her word) their Russian hosts into subservience. Her 'battering-ram technique' carried all before them; Marutha would have been proud of her.

Thus, the bond between brother and sister was reforged. Critics said that Yehudi sometimes insisted that Hephzibah accompany him at recitals out of a feeling of family loyalty; otherwise, they said, her own concert career might have been a little sketchy. The same critics have since levelled the same accusation against Yehudi's son, Jeremy, whose appearances lately under his father's baton are in part a desire by Yehudi to relive that earlier, glorious partnership. (Yaltah was also an accomplished pianist, incidentally, although her physical frailty has prevented her from achieving what she might have done. Yehudi always maintains that Yaltah has 'remarkable musicality ... less commanding of the keyboard [than Hephzibah], but her performances are more revealing'.)

But such criticism misses the mark. Yehudi's performances with all his family are often, as we have seen, attempts to re-experience the golden moments of his childhood. In a striking passage in his autobiography, Yehudi suddenly lists all those qualities which he says Hephzibah has in common with Marutha – 'balanced, methodical and [so] reliable that when confronted with a duty she will do it, unaffected by the pressures of immediate past or immediate future ... [Hephzibah] abhors exaggeration, and her playing has a clean, clear, somewhat no-nonsense approach, abjuring frills. It has as little cosmetic as she has, as little patience with the gaudy, eye-catching gesture as she herself is free of ambition to attract attention.'

But these qualities are a long way from the real Marutha, as both Yaltah and Hephzibah had come to realize. For years, however, Yehudi, the son, continued to love his mother deeply, and continued to believe that Hephzibah had 'found utter fulfilment in her life, her husband, and her own music, and wore self-discipline, not as a rein upon an explosive temperament, but with joyful equanimity. She had nothing to suppress,' Yehudi added. Marutha, on the other hand, had certainly not worn her self-discipline 'with joyful equanimity'. Too late Yehudi discovered that Hephzibah was riddled with self-doubt just as she was becoming increasingly riddled with cancer. Too late he was forced to admit that 'she was not self-propelled. She needed an object of inspiration, *preferably her brother* [my italics]. She required other people's conviction to bolster her own; her character permitted self-assertiveness only in a larger cause.' We now know what Hephzibah had attempted to suppress; her letters speak eloquently of 'the wreckage'. We know too that this attempt, with its desperate struggle to reconcile fact with fantasy, had been doomed from the beginning.

A year after Hephzibah's death, Moshe died. From the moment Yehudi had finally left home – at Nola's insistence – Moshe's entire life had lost its purpose. No more interviews, no more management of the finances, just his avocados and his tomatoes, his plums and his oranges, the flowers in his 'own Jerusalem at Los Gatos'. He had begun to write – he was, after all, an established Hebrew scholar – in particular about what he saw as the failure of Israel to become the Promised Land. It was now so concerned with military and territorial matters, he said, that its spiritual purpose had been forgotten. Eventually he wrote a book entitled *The Decadence of Judaism in our Time*. It caused an uproar in Israel, not least because Moshe was Yehudi's father. As a result of the book, 'his people hated him,' Marutha told me. 'He was controversial with the Jewish people because he had told them the truth.' Referring to some vast Jewish conspiracy which has obviously grown in Marutha's mind, she claimed that the book was 'taken out of the libraries. It disappeared. My husband was persecuted by the Zionist movement to such an extent that finally he got cancer. Our family was maligned! And the stress caused the cancer.' When Marutha told me this in Yehudi's presence, Yehudi immediately protested that the causal connection between reaction to the book and the cancer from which Moshe died was less than certain. 'There you are,' Marutha said to me triumphantly. 'That's typical Yehudi. Always trying to find a diplomatic solution. But it's a fact. He was killed by his own people.' Later, Yehudi told me again about the death of Hephzibah: 'I admit it. It was her life that killed her,' he said.

Like all the Menuhins, Moshe was a wonderful storyteller. The aural tradition of the Jews of the Pale was still within living memory. A favourite story concerned an ancestor named Benjamin who was, inevitably, a fiddler. Benjamin also possessed a voice 'so golden that one's heart melted in sweetness and adoration'. As a result, he was frequently called upon to sing at weddings as well as other, less formal celebrations. One such was a drunken party given by the local landowner, a debauch which apparently had continued for several days and nights. Benjamin, no doubt as drunk as the rest, had been persuaded to put on a bearskin and perform like a dancing bear. Eventually, said Moshe, he had been thrown into a huge barrel of water and ordered to continue singing. Benjamin had seemed to love every minute of it and sang away at the top of his voice. He had been rewarded by the landowner, whose party it was, with a new brick house. When he had come to his senses, however, and returned sober to the rabbi under whom he was studying the Talmud, Benjamin had been so disgusted by his behaviour that he had trampled on his violin and vowed to spend the rest of his life singing holy prayers in penance. 'It does not become a Jew to fiddle while his people are in exile,' he had said.

Yehudi is a fiddler who has been 'singing holy prayers' with his violin his entire life in penance for the transgressions of his parents. In the beginning, this was clearly instinctive. But later, as reality crashed down upon him, he saw that these holy prayers were threatened. Yaltah, and later Hephzibah, realized the truth before him, but were not strong enough to do anything. Yehudi, however, was tougher; much tougher. Sensing that he now had a mission, he transformed these holy prayers into concern for a universal brotherhood, just as Hephzibah's character had ultimately 'permitted self-assertiveness only in a larger cause'.

The tragedy of Yehudi's life has been the extent to which he has been unable to reconcile myth with reality. One might argue that he was never given much of a chance. One of his very first reviews, for instance, was from Irving Weil. Writing in the *New York Journal,* he said: 'If you had closed your eyes, you would immediately have lost the picture of the rather fat little youngster in blouse and knickers and bare knees, with his fiddle to his chin, staunchly bowing away in front of the orchestra.' Of all the early reviews that I have been able to find (and Moshe kept most of them, in enormous scrapbooks), only Richard Stokes, contributing to the *New York Evening World,* observed something odd, although this must have been more by luck than judgement. '[Yehudi's] method appears to me faulty,' Stokes wrote, 'in that the violin is permitted to slope down from the shoulder, instead of being flung aloft ... while the tone is dependent wholly on strength of bowing, instead of partly on the pressure of the fingers of the left hand.'

Considerations of violin technique apart, it was an ominous warning. No matter that elsewhere Stokes said that Yehudi was 'well-nigh supernatural, plunging the hearer into metaphysical speculations as to the theory of reincarnation'. No matter that the *Brooklyn Eagle* said that 'one is inclined to doubt Yehudi's mortality'. Like his ancestor Benjamin, Yehudi was being condemned to an eventual ducking in a barrel. At one of his early concerts in San Francisco, he had been presented in the interval with a box of flowers. The hysteria at the end of the concert had been so great that every single flower (as well as items from Yehudi's clothes) was torn from his hands by a mob desperate for souvenirs.

Yet, as we know, Yehudi survived. Indeed, many of his daredevil feats during the Second World War seem almost as if he were consciously challenging this supposed immortality. Groping around in the blackout of London; spending nights in the underground stations playing for the homeless; determined to land on the beaches of Normandy with the Allies (he actually landed less than a week after the advance troops); performing in Antwerp while part of the city was still occupied by the German army – in fact, he insisted on playing while he could hear Antwerp being bombarded by the retreating Nazis; giving a memorable concert at the Paris Opéra with Charles Munch and the Conservatoire Symphony Orchestra while Paris was still half-deserted; thereafter crash-landing his plane from Paris in a field in Kent (because the landing gear had jammed), in order to make a promised BBC broadcast in London.

His prodigious efforts to correct what he himself came to accept was a faulty violin technique ('no scales and arpeggi') have been documented earlier – 'I felt like a marionette being pulled back,' he remembered, 'the strings manipulated by a senseless cruel force.' That he struggled to solve the problem himself, and did not abandon hope as many other violinists finding themselves in not dissimilar situations have done, says volumes about the man. He realized that playing the violin was 'dependent on the moral and physical condition of the musician. [The violin] is a far more elusive instrument to reduce to terms of cold technique than, say, the piano.'

He has also survived personal attacks, the most strident (and hurtful) of which was in December 1945 when Ira A. Hirschmann, founder president of the New Friends of Music in New York, announced that he was 'horror-stricken' that Yehudi was 'attempting to whitewash the Nazi official musical director of the Third

Reich, Wilhelm Furtwängler ... That anyone should give a clean bill of health to one of their conspirators seems incredible ... we are outraged!' However much Yehudi had felt justified in supporting Furtwängler, the attack stung him deeply. 'Go on, play for the murderers,' shouted one heckler at a concert. 'I've come to you as a Jew,' Yehudi replied, 'to tell you what I've done, I've done as a Jew.'

I had an unexpected insight into the immense struggle that has gone on, late one night in what was then East Berlin. I was on tour with Yehudi and Diana, in part to commemorate the sixtieth anniversary of his first appearance in Berlin and Dresden. On this occasion, he was conducting and not playing. Characteristically, he had decided to stay on after the scheduled rehearsal in the evening to do some extra work. I had had enough, and decided to return to our hotel. Awaiting me was a note from Diana, asking me to join them for supper in their suite. I arrived and explained that Yehudi was still at work. 'Oh, typical,' she said, and told me to help myself to a drink, and a large vodka for herself.

'Oh, if only you knew what I've had to endure,' she said suddenly. (I should explain that I am not exactly a close family friend, so this sudden confidence took me aback.) 'We were both of us so ambitious; we had such terrific aspirations. And now we are both so aware of how little we've actually done. I keep trying to persuade Yehudi to take a sabbatical, for instance. He did once, when he was almost sixty. He wrote that autobiography, but he never seemed to stop the entire year. He doesn't read, as I do. Never has time. Once, I remember, he got stuck in some terrible little town in Montana, and the only book he had was by Dostoevsky – *From the House of the Dead*. Typical.

'Nothing seems to throw him off his stride,' Diana went on. 'I remember being amazed at some of the early concerts I went to as his wife. It didn't matter *what* happened, he somehow kept going. He was playing the Bartók Second Violin Concerto, for example, when the conductor accidentally whacked Yehudi's Stradivarius with his baton. Yehudi merely raised the violin to protect himself. At the same concert – it was sponsored, I think, by the Daughters of the American Revolution – there was a woman with an enormous bosom sitting near the front carrying a large balloon. Sure enough, at a particularly delicate moment, the balloon went pop. I thought the whole thing had been a disaster, and afterwards I went round to the dressing room to make sure that at least Yehudi and the Stradivarius had survived. There was this woman with her burst balloon, complaining. 'Oh, I'm terribly sorry,' said Yehudi. 'I *do* beg your pardon.' 'And the Stradivarius?' I said. 'Oh, that's all right,' said Yehudi. 'I only missed about two bars, I think.'

To this day, Diana still travels everywhere with Yehudi on tour. Air travel is now essential for their crazy schedule, but air travel makes her as nervous as a kitten. She always insists on sitting in the front row, whatever the class ('nearest the exit'), and chatters the entire journey. She is nurse and mother and wife; their devotion to each other is absolute; without her, Yehudi would be lost. At lunch she will carefully arrange his daily intake of vitamin pills, lest he forget; granoton, rich in vitamin C; biostrath, a Swiss concoction made from yeast; molat, vitamin B; ginseng; herb tea – 'horrid, the lot of them,' Diana tells me cheerily. She buys his shirts, his ties and his shoes; when he occasionally risks a purchase on his own, he is likely to incur her displeasure. If he appears for a television interview, she will supervise his appearance and often – in the presence of a somewhat confused camera crew – order him from the room to 'change his shirt into something more appropriate'. And, of course, she combs his hair.

'It's been my job to protect him,' Diana went on, clutching another vodka. 'Not just from the bad reviews, or from those who would abuse his time. But from himself. As I told you before, he has no wall to back against. If you push him, he'll just fall over and disappear from view. Smashed into pieces, like Humpty-Dumpty. He likes to drift. Because his role is different, and I think that in some mystical way he understood this as a child. I feel on occasions that I am the stoker in the boiler room keeping the SS *Menuhin* afloat, while Yehudi is the captain on the bridge gazing at the inspiring view. The Indians have what they call the Bodhisattva, a demi-God who passes messages from the Gods to human beings. *That's* what Yehudi is.

'But you have to shore him up all the time,' Diana said, 'to make him feel that he is what he is. Music, for him, is an art of time. It carries him from A to B in so many minutes and hours. He lives that time through the composer's imagination, with all of that composer's emotions and wisdom. It is both liberating and yet profoundly dangerous, because it removes him from any sense of reality. Thus he can never condemn, can never shut a door, can never throw an envelope away, can never believe that something is not first-rate, never believe that anyone is taking advantage of him. It's been my job to prevent him from becoming completely disillusioned, because without his illusions he would be shattered. Most of us have that problem,' Diana added, 'but with Yehudi it is a matter of life and death.'

Marutha, Nola (if only briefly), and now Diana. The child he is closest to is Zamira, his daughter. His sisters Hephzibah and Yaltah. All women; all protecting him. Marutha from the torments of what she must have known was her inadequate marriage; Nola, from what she perceived as his marauding parents; Zamira, from her alcoholic mother and what she believed might be the consequences of that on Yehudi's already uneasy psyche; Diana, from the knowledge which disillusion would bring; Yaltah, from the truth about their mother. And Hephzibah?

When Hephzibah died, Yehudi had wanted to put away his violin, vowing never to play again. He did, occasionally, but the fire had gone out. The performance he gave of the Beethoven Violin Concerto in Moscow after her death was mesmerizing. It was out-of-tune, technically a mess, and musically embarrassing. Only in the second movement did the man shine through, and then with a message painful to hear. His performance spoke of loneliness and desolation and a terrible spiritual emptiness. Hephzibah had been the last secure link to a childhood that, if not golden, shone in his imagination as a true moment of happiness. Yaltah could no longer be trusted; Marutha had her own memories, now locked away for ever. Throughout his long life, others had come and gone, and sometimes given Yehudi profound pleasure. But with Hephzibah, 'my Siamese soul', there had been something else. And now she was dead.

Diana often cites the Indian Bodhisattva as a way of describing Yehudi's apparent unworldliness. According to the teachings of Buddha, such beings practise the works of paramita, that is, good deeds to others; just like Yehudi. The Buddha himself had been reincarnated as a Bodhisattva, in the guise of a golden swan who, when he glided over the water, had glowed like the full moon; just like Yehudi. What Diana does not mention is that the Bodhisattva is also someone who, before entering into full enlightenment, is obliged to travel a road full of pain and suffering. Yehudi Menuhin has certainly travelled such a road.

Index

YM stands for Yehudi Menuhin

Index

Index